Unshrink Yourself

*12 Mini-Shifts to Ditch Self-Doubt
and Own Your Life*

Thanh Nguyen

Dedication

To my beautiful daughter and son, who remind me every day of who I need to be — unapologetically me.

To my husband, for his unwavering support and encouragement to follow my path.

Praise for
Unshrink Yourself

"If you've ever held yourself back, played small when you knew you had more to give, or wondered whether your voice really matters, **this book is for you.** It will remind you that the world doesn't need a smaller version of you—it needs the fullest, boldest, most authentic expression of you."

– Jack Canfield, Co-creator, *Chicken Soup for the Soul*® series and New York Times Bestselling Author, *The Success Principles™: How to Get from Where You Are to Where You Want to Be*

*"**Unshrink Yourself** helps readers grow into confident, values-driven leaders.** Thanh Nguyen is a shining example of the Maxwell Leadership mission in action — to equip and empower others to lead with integrity, purpose, and passion. She embodies what it means to add value to people."

— **Chris Robinson,** Executive Vice President of Maxwell Leadership Team and USA Today Bestselling Author, *From Drift to Drive: A High Achiever's Guide To Breaking The Chains Of Complacency*

Table of Contents

Foreword

When I began my journey of teaching people how to live with purpose, take bold action, and achieve their dreams, I realized something essential: success doesn't begin with circumstances; it begins with confidence. Without confidence, even the most talented people hesitate. They wait for permission, they shrink from opportunities, and they let fear dictate their future. With confidence, ordinary people accomplish extraordinary things.

That's why this book is so important. In *Unshrink Yourself*, Thanh Nguyen gives you a roadmap to build confidence from the inside out. She doesn't talk about confidence as a performance or a mask you put on. Instead, she shows you how to create it through what she calls mini-shifts—small, doable changes in the way you think, speak, and act that compound over time into extraordinary transformation.

I love Thanh's approach because it's grounded in both wisdom and action. She weaves in her own personal stories about moments of fear, doubt, and imposter syndrome alongside proven strategies anyone can use. Each chapter doesn't just inspire you; it equips you with practical steps, reflection questions, and exercises that help you turn insight into habit.

What I admire most about Thanh is that she has lived this work. She knows what it means to face adversity, to doubt yourself, and to rise stronger. Her journey is a testament to the truth that confidence is not something you're born with; it's something you build, one decision at a time.

If you've ever held yourself back, played small when you knew you had more to give, or wondered whether your voice matters, this book is for you. It will remind you that the world doesn't need a smaller version of you; it needs the fullest, boldest, most authentic expression of you.

So, read this book with an open heart. Try the exercises. Take the mini-shifts seriously. I promise you, if you apply what Thanh shares here, you won't just think differently; you'll live differently. You'll speak up when you once stayed silent. You'll step forward when you once held back. You'll unshrink yourself.

And when you do, you'll not only transform your own life; you'll inspire everyone around you to rise higher too.

Co-creator, *Chicken Soup for the Soul®* series
New York Times Bestselling Author, *The Success Principles™: How to Get from Where You Are to Where You Want to Be*

A Note on the Cover

In September 2025, I had the opportunity to accompany 140 Maxwell Leadership Certified Coaches on a Transformation Trip to Argentina, where we provided values-based leadership roundtable training to over 5,000 facilitators. It was an incredible experience of growth, service, and connection. The journey reminded me how transformation often begins with a single step of willingness to give and grow.

During that trip, I visited Iguazú National Park, where the waterfalls cascade with both power and grace. Water has always fascinated me because it's soft, yet unstoppable. It finds its way around every obstacle, flowing with persistence and purpose. It represents how we can move through life's challenges, not always by resisting, but by allowing ourselves to flow, adapt, and grow.

Amid that breathtaking scenery, I saw a small butterfly resting quietly — the 88 butterfly (Diaethria clymena). Its wings carry a natural pattern shaped like the number 88, a symbol of balance, transformation, and infinite potential. I instinctively reached for my camera and captured its image right there. That photo later became the cover of this book.

That butterfly reminded me that each of us is beautifully unique, designed exactly as we are meant to be. When we stop shrinking, doubting, or hiding, and instead offer our strength, authenticity, and love to the world, we not only serve others better, but we also honor who we truly are.

May this butterfly remind you, as it reminded me, that **you were never meant to shrink.**

You were meant to **rise, shine, and flow, just as you are.**

INTRODUCTION:
You're Not Alone

The lights were bright, almost blinding. Hundreds of faces stared back at me, waiting. My heart hammered so loudly I was sure the people in the front row could hear it. I had prepared for weeks, rehearsing in the mirror until my words felt like second nature, but in that moment, standing for the first time in front of the entire company, my palms were slick with sweat.

And butterflies in my stomach? More like a storm.

As I gripped the podium, I willed my voice not to betray the nerves inside me. For a split second, I wanted to shrink, to make myself smaller, to disappear into the crowd. *Who am I to stand here?* I thought. *What if I fail?*

But then came the shift. A quiet but steady voice whispered inside me: *You belong here. You've done the work. Breathe. Speak.*

I opened my mouth. And instead of trembling, my voice carried. It wasn't perfect, but it was powerful. Each sentence grew steadier, each breath deeper. I didn't just deliver a talk that day — I stepped into a new version of myself.

***

My first public speaking event came exactly 20 years ago. I had been invited to give a talk during our company's weekly Friday lunch to share about a product development milestone. It was an honor, but a terrifying one.

That talk, my first company-wide presentation, happened because of something I'd started months earlier: joining Toastmasters. Toastmasters was where I first learned to speak up, even when my hands trembled and my vision blurred. Week after week, I stood in front of a small group, stumbling through introductions, learning to breathe, to pause, to connect. Little by little, the fear loosened its grip. My voice grew steadier. I was no longer invisible. I was noticed at work as someone with potential. So when I was later asked to give that company presentation, I said yes, still scared, but ready. That was the beginning of my journey with confidence. Not the end of fear, but the start of learning how to rise above it.

Diving into Mini-Shifts, Rebuilding, and Imposter Syndrome

Confidence isn't built through grand transformations or overnight makeovers. It grows in what I call **mini-shifts** – small, intentional changes that may seem minor in the moment but that accumulate into something life-changing.

A shift is both a movement and a momentum. A shift changes your direction. Even the tiniest shift, like a plane adjusting its course by just one degree, can alter the destination. In the same way, one mini-shift in your thinking, your words, or your actions can change the trajectory of your confidence and your life.

If you've ever struggled with self-confidence, doubted yourself, second-guessed your decisions, or felt like an imposter in your own life, **you are not alone.** You are in good company. Despite what social media might suggest, self-confidence isn't something people are just born with. It's not reserved for the lucky few who are always bold, fearless, or naturally self-assured. It's something we *all* have to build and rebuild over time.

Yes, you read that right: **rebuild.** You might feel confident in one season of life, only to question yourself in the next. A major transition, a new role, or an unfamiliar challenge can shake even the strongest self-belief. Confidence isn't a permanent state; this practice adapts as we grow.

***

Even the most successful people you admire have wrestled with fear, doubt, and insecurity.

In 1999, Hillary Clinton was considering running for U.S. Senate in New York. She was already a high-profile figure as First Lady of the United States. But running for office herself? That was a different story.

She was afraid she might lose. She questioned if she could handle the spotlight, the pressure, and the possibility of failure. So, she turned to a friend, Betsy Wright, and confessed her fears. Her friend listened and said four words that would change everything: "Hillary, dare to compete."

Those words stayed with her. She later wrote, *"I realized that fear of failing shouldn't stop me from trying."* So she ran. And she won.

She became the first, first lady to hold elected office, opening the door to a new chapter of leadership. What made her move forward wasn't the absence of fear but the presence of purpose. She knew what mattered to her, and that became stronger than her fear.

And that's what I want for you.

❝

We often mistake confidence for charisma, loudness, or ease in the spotlight. We think it means being the most outspoken person in the room or never feeling nervous before a big moment. But real confidence is quieter. It's not about shouting how great you are - it's about knowing who you are, even when no one is watching.

Maya Angelou, the legendary writer and poet, once said, "I have written eleven books, but each time I think, 'Uh oh, they're going to find out now. I've run a game on everybody, and they're going to find me out.'" This is **imposter syndrome** – a term coined by psychologists Pauline Clance and Suzanne Imes – a silent thief of confidence that whispers: *You're not good enough. You don't belong here. Who do you think you are?*

And Maya Angelou was not alone in this.

Adele, one of the most celebrated singers of our time, has admitted to severe anxiety before performances. She often has panic attacks and struggles with stage fright. Yet, she walks out on stage again and again, not because she's fearless, but because she's anchored in her love for music and her truth.

Emma Watson, who grew up on camera as Hermione in *Harry Potter*, confessed that she often felt she didn't deserve her platform as a United Nations Goodwill Ambassador. She said, "I felt like an imposter. I thought, 'Who am I to speak for women around the world?'"

And Michelle Obama, someone many people look up to as the epitome of grace and strength, once said: "I still have a little imposter syndrome. It doesn't go away, that feeling that you shouldn't take me that seriously. What do I know?"

If these powerful women, authors, artists, activists, and leaders can feel afraid or unworthy at times, maybe there's nothing wrong with *you* for feeling that way, too. Maybe confidence isn't about never doubting yourself. Maybe it's about what you do *despite* those doubts.

Confidence from the Inside Out

A kindred soul asked me the other day how I quiet the negative voices in my head so I can have the courage to grow and do what I'm meant to do. I laughed. Because I've never been able to quiet those voices. I carry them with me like a baby on my hip. They whisper:

You're not good enough.

People will laugh at you.

You'll embarrass yourself.

And yet, I act anyway.

Before every talk, I feel stage fright. But then another voice rises: *Thanh, these people gave you their most precious gift, which is their time. You're here to serve. So go out there and give them everything you've got.* That voice of purpose doesn't erase fear. But it walks beside it.

"

Fear and courage are like yin and yang. Like the lotus that blooms from the mud, your doubts and your dreams can coexist. You don't have to silence the fear to take the next step – you just have to decide which voice you'll listen to.

You don't build confidence by pretending to be fearless. You build it by taking small, meaningful steps even when you're afraid. You don't build it by waiting for others to approve of you. You build it by learning to trust yourself.

You don't build it by puffing yourself up with only affirmations. You build it by aligning your actions with your **values,** with what you care about, who you want to be, and what life you want to live.

When you live in alignment with your values, even in small ways, confidence naturally follows. Because you're not trying to be someone else. You're becoming more of who you *already are.*

This Book Is Your Starting Point

In the pages that follow, you'll find 12 practical, powerful mini-shifts to help you build real, lasting confidence from the inside out. These aren't gimmicks. They're not about 'acting' confident or faking it till you make it. They're small, doable shifts that help you:

- Accept praise instead of deflecting it
- Clarify your core values so you can live with integrity
- Embrace your authenticity so you can bring your best, unique self to serve the world
- Know what you want and pursue it
- Understand your passion, mission, and why you do what you do
- Learn how to take small forward actions, even if they are imperfect
- Talk to yourself as if you are talking to your most precious, loving, younger version of yourself
- Focus on running your own race to win the race that matters to you
- Celebrate the wins, whether they are large or small
- Align your breath, body, and mind to work for you
- Embrace failure as a step to learning and winning
- Find a network of friends and advocates who celebrate you and cheer you on

Each chapter includes a story, a why-it-matters explanation, reflection questions or exercises, and a small to-do action that you can take right away. And you don't have to do it all at once.

You don't have to feel confident *before* you begin – you just have to begin.

Let's Walk This Path Together

If you've ever felt like you weren't enough...

If you've ever stayed quiet when you wanted to speak...

If you've ever watched someone else succeed and wondered, *Why not me?* ...

I wrote this for you.

I've been there too. I've wrestled with fear and silence and uncertainty. But I've also discovered tools, truths, and daily practices that helped me find my voice, and I want to share them with you because the world needs your voice. Your gifts. Your leadership. Not someday, but now. Confidence isn't the absence of fear. It's the decision to keep moving forward in the presence of it.

Let's take that next step together.

How to Read This Book

I invite you to read this book in the way that works best for you. You can approach this book in two ways:

Option 1: Quick Read, Then Deep Dive

Start by reading the entire book in one sitting, but skip the Suggested Action Steps for now.

Then, go back to the chapters that resonate most with you. This time, dive into the Action Steps and put them into practice, because real change happens only when we take action. That's how we reshape our habits, shift our thinking, and create success.

Option 2: One Chapter at a Time

Read one chapter per week and focus on the Action Steps. Don't feel pressured to do them all at once. Choose just one step to work on. One small step forward is all it takes to keep moving in the right direction.

No matter which way you choose, remember: transformation isn't about perfection, but about steady, intentional steps that lead you closer to the life you want.

Why Confidence Matters More Than You Think

True self-confidence is more than a fleeting feeling. It's a grounded, resilient belief in your ability to face challenges, make decisions, and succeed. The quiet voice inside says, *I can figure this out*, even when you don't have all the answers yet.

It's not about being loud or having all the answers, but trusting your own capacity to navigate what comes your way.

And in a world that's constantly changing and filled with uncertainty and noise, that belief might be the most important thing you can cultivate.

It's natural to think that competence leads to confidence, but the relationship often goes the other way around, because confidence leads to competence. You have to believe you can do something before you're willing to try, learn, and improve at it.

A meta-analysis, which is a study that gathers and analyzes findings from many other studies to uncover the bigger truth, by Alexander D. Stajkovic and Fred Luthans (1998) found something powerful: people who believe in themselves usually perform better. Confidence matters. Even when someone isn't the most skilled person in the room, their belief in their ability often gives them the edge.

> **❝**
>
> *Why? Because **belief unlocks action.** **And action unlocks ability.***

When you show up with confidence, you access more of your potential. It is not because you're perfect, but because you're willing to begin. You raise your hand. You volunteer. You try. *That's* when growth happens.

The research of Albert Bandura, the pioneer of self-efficacy theory, shows that people with high self-confidence view challenges as opportunities to learn, rather than threats to avoid. They don't interpret failure as a reflection of who they are. Instead, they see it as part of the process.

When you believe you can figure things out, you're more likely to stay in the game. You'll persist through difficulties, bounce back from rejection, and keep working toward your goals. And that persistence, much more than talent, is often the determining factor in long-term success.

When Confidence Is Missing: The Hidden Cost

Low self-confidence doesn't just hold you back. It actively undermines your potential.

In 1978, psychologists Pauline Clance and Suzanne Imes coined the term imposter syndrome, a term that describes high achievers who, despite evidence of their competence, feel like frauds. They attribute success to luck, timing, or the mistakes of others. Impostor syndrome is linked to anxiety, burnout, self-sabotage, and missed opportunities.

Studies suggest that up to 70 percent of people experience impostor feelings in their careers (Sakulku & Alexander, 2011). When your inner voice is full of doubt, you might hesitate to speak up, shrink from leadership opportunities, or overwork yourself trying to prove you belong. You're not alone—many high achievers feel this way, even when their success is clear to everyone else.

The result? Emotional exhaustion, lost opportunities, and an unfulfilled sense of potential – not because you weren't capable, but because you didn't believe you were.

The Confidence Gap: A Gendered Reality

A now-famous internal Hewlett-Packard report revealed that men usually apply for a job when they meet 60% of the qualifications. Women? They wait until they meet 100%.

That gap isn't about ability; it's about belief.

In their 2014 article and book by the same name (The Confidence Code), Katty Kay and Claire Shipman called this phenomenon the Confidence Gap. They argue that social conditioning, perfectionism, and internalized bias often lead women to underestimate themselves, even when their track records are equal to or better than their male counterparts.

I remember a moment early in my engineering career that brought this to life. During a conversation with one of my coworkers, another woman engineer, I was praising a male colleague on his recent promotion, talking about how smart and capable he was. She stopped me mid-sentence and asked, "Why do you think he's better than you? What credentials or experiences does he have that you don't?"

I froze. I had never really considered that. He had less experience, fewer credentials, and had taken on easier projects than I had. Yet somehow, he was confident enough to ask for that promotion, the one I secretly wished for but never believed I deserved. And guess what? He got it. Not because he was more qualified, but because he asked.

The implication is clear: confidence isn't just a personal matter; it's a cultural one. And reclaiming it isn't just good for individual women but is essential for more equitable workplaces, leadership tables, and innovation teams.

Confidence Affects Your Well-Being

Confidence isn't just good for your goals; it's also good for your health.

People with higher self-confidence report lower rates of anxiety and depression. They're more likely to engage in healthy behaviors, manage stress effectively, and maintain fulfilling relationships. They sleep better, handle criticism with more resilience, and recover faster from setbacks.

Why? Because they're not constantly second-guessing their worth or replaying every misstep. They have an inner belief that they can navigate life's ups and downs with strength and self-trust.

The Nature vs. Nurture vs. Self-Built Debate

Confidence, like many traits, is influenced by multiple factors – your biology, your upbringing, and your choices. Researchers have long debated how much each component contributes, and while there's no universally agreed-upon percentage, modern psychology gives us a solid approximation:

Factor	Approximate Contribution*	Explanation
Genetics (Nature)	~30–40%	Personality traits we're born with, such as how outgoing, calm, or emotionally sensitive we are, shape our starting point for confidence.
Environment (Nurture)	~30–40%	Parenting, culture, education, trauma, and role models all shape our beliefs and sense of self.
Within Our Control (Learnable)	~20–40%	Confidence is highly trainable through action, mindset shifts, affirmations, and mastering challenges.

* These are suggested ranges for narrative purposes, not rigid numbers.

The Role of Genetics

Some of us are born a little bolder; others, a little quieter. Twin studies show that genetics account for about 30 to 50 percent of the differences in self-esteem and confidence. That means part of our temperament, whether we lean toward shyness or sociability, is written in our DNA.

But genes are only the opening scene, not the whole story.

Growing up, I was the quiet one. I preferred to listen rather than speak. In meetings, my mind was full of ideas, but my lips stayed sealed. I thought confidence was something people were born with and that I just didn't have that gene.

But over the years, I learned that while temperament may shape how we start, it doesn't define how far we can go. Each time I raised my hand, spoke up, or volunteered for a project that scared me, I built a little more courage. Confidence, I realized, is like a muscle, part nature, part nurture, and largely learnable.

The Power of Environment

Our environment, especially in childhood and adolescence, plays a huge role in shaping our self-confidence. The messages we receive from parents, teachers, culture, and media become internal narratives: *You're capable.* Or... *You'll never be enough.*

For example, a child praised for effort instead of perfection usually develops a growth mindset, which fuels confidence in adulthood. Meanwhile, those raised in overly critical or neglectful environments may internalize self-doubt.

None of us build confidence in a vacuum. Our environment matters. Our upbringing matters. The words we hear and the ones we internalize matter deeply.

If you grew up in a culture that discouraged risk-taking, self-expression, or self-celebration, you may have absorbed the belief that confidence is dangerous or arrogant.

But now you get to choose differently.

You get to unlearn the scripts that no longer serve you and write a new story. One rooted not in fear, but in possibility.

What You Can Control: Confidence Is Learnable

The most empowering insight? Confidence is a skill.

You don't need to be born with it. You can build it intentionally, consistently, and strategically.

Albert Bandura's theory of self-efficacy shows that belief in our ability grows through:

- Mastery experiences – succeeding at challenges
- Representation experiences – seeing others like us succeed
- Social persuasion – receiving encouragement
- Emotional regulation – calming nerves to perform well

Similarly, Carol Dweck's growth mindset research proves that when people believe their abilities can grow, they're more confident and resilient.

If you've ever thought, "I'm just not a confident person," it's time to challenge that belief. Confidence may start with biology and be shaped by environment, but it can absolutely be rebuilt and grown again and again through conscious effort.

I've seen it in myself. I've seen it in the professionals I coach. And if you're reading this, it's likely that you've already built more confidence than you give yourself credit for.

You don't have to wait until you feel confident to take action. The feeling often comes after the doing. Every time you show up scared but willing, speak up despite trembling, or rise after a failure, you're practicing confidence. And practice makes it your default.

> **"**
>
> *Confidence isn't something you find. It's something you build; one choice, one breath, one brave moment at a time.*

And you, without question, can build it.

Confidence Is Not Arrogance

Let's clear up a common misconception: confidence is not arrogance.

Arrogance is rooted in insecurity. It's loud, defensive, and often dismissive of others. It needs to prove superiority.

Confidence is rooted in self-trust. It's open, curious, and unthreatened by other people's strengths. It allows space for growth and welcomes collaboration.

A confident person doesn't need to be the smartest in the room. They're wise enough to ask questions and secure enough to share the spotlight.

In his book *Good to Great*, Jim Collins calls this "Level 5 Leadership" — a blend of humility and fierce determination.

When Darwin Smith became CEO of Kimberly-Clark in 1971, the company was struggling. Instead of pretending to have all the answers, he spent time asking questions and listening. Many expected a charismatic, bold leader, but Smith was quiet and self-effacing. When he made the radical decision to sell the company's paper mills and focus on consumer products like Kleenex and Huggies, critics thought he was crazy.

But Smith wasn't driven by ego; he said, "I never stopped trying to become qualified for the job." His humility and willingness to learn transformed Kimberly-Clark into one of the most successful consumer goods companies in the world.

Confidence Is the Core of Leadership

Leadership without confidence is like a GPS with no signal. You can have all the knowledge in the world, but if you can't trust your own judgment, make decisions, or lead others through uncertainty, you'll struggle to lead.

"

People don't just follow competence; they follow conviction.

Confident leaders inspire trust, model resilience, and create psychological safety. They don't have to pretend to know it all. Their humility often enhances their confidence. They admit mistakes, ask questions, and give credit freely.

Because true confidence doesn't shout. It doesn't bully. It doesn't dominate.

It listens. It learns. And it leads with calm, quiet power.

Every Comeback Starts with Confidence

Behind every great success story is a moment of doubt, a turning point where someone chose to believe in themselves anyway.

Oprah Winfrey was told she was unfit for TV. Michael Jordan was cut from his high school basketball team. J.K. Rowling's first *Harry Potter* manuscript was rejected 12 times.

What made them different wasn't luck. It was their quiet refusal to give up, a belief that their story wasn't over.

That's what confidence gives you: the power to keep going. The courage to try again. The resilience to rise after every fall.

Confidence Grows with a Growth Mindset

Psychologist Carol Dweck introduced a growth mindset, the belief that your abilities can be developed through effort, learning, and persistence. First popularized in her 2006 book *Mindset: The New Psychology of Success*, Dweck's decades of research at Stanford showed that people with a growth mindset see failure as feedback, not a verdict, and approach challenges with curiosity rather than fear. That mindset shift changes everything. When you stop believing that ability is fixed, you start allowing yourself room to grow. You try new things. You seek feedback. You bounce back faster. Over time, your belief in your ability to grow becomes confidence itself.

"

*In other words: **confidence isn't built on being perfect, it's built on being willing.***

Confidence fuels action. Action builds experience. Experience creates competence. And competence reinforces confidence.

This is the upward spiral that changes lives. Every small win becomes evidence that you're capable, and that evidence rewires your brain and strengthens your belief in yourself.

This is why confident people often rise faster and farther. It's not that they're better; it's that they're braver. They take the shot. They ask the question. They go for the opportunity before they feel 100% ready.

And in doing so, they build real capacity with one stretch, one risk, one step at a time.

MINI-SHIFT #1:

Own Your Light

"When we are pushing away compliments, we are pushing away connection."

– Brené Brown

I stared at the blank Testimonials section of my new speaker website. I could hear my speaking coach's voice from our last conversation:

"Do you have any testimonials from your past talks that you could share?"

Testimonials.

The word itself stirred something inside me.

Then I remembered — the stack.

Buried in a drawer somewhere was a bundle of thank-you notes from the time I spoke at the University of Idaho more than a decade ago. It was my very first talk, in front of nearly two hundred students. I had shared my story of coming to America from Vietnam, of facing abuse, language barriers, cultural shock, and self-doubt, and how I learned to rise above both external and internal limitations.

A few days after the event, my friend, the professor who had invited me, mailed me a thick envelope filled with handwritten notes from his students. I remembered tucking them away carefully, as if they were something precious. And somehow, over the years, I had carried them with me, even through two moves, across 3,000 miles, and through multiple chapters of life, without ever opening them.

I opened the drawer slowly. There they were: dozens of envelopes tied together with a faded rubber band, their edges yellowed by time. I held them in my hands and felt a strange tightening in my chest. My fingers brushed the rough paper, but I couldn't bring myself to untie the bundle.

I was afraid.

Not afraid of criticism, but of kindness. I knew those letters were filled with encouragement, admiration, and gratitude because after my talk, the students had lined up for more than an hour long to talk to me, thanking me and sharing how my story inspired them and gave them hope.

But I wasn't ready to believe it.

Somewhere deep down, a quiet voice whispered: You don't deserve this.

So, I put the stack back in the drawer and shut it again.

Do you ever struggle to accept compliments?

I used to do it all the time. For years, I thought that brushing off compliments was a form of humility. If someone said, "You look nice," I'd smile awkwardly and say, "Oh, this old thing?"

If someone told me, "You're smart," I'd reply, "I was just lucky." Sound familiar?

I didn't realize it, but I was unknowingly reinforcing a belief that I didn't deserve recognition. I thought I was being modest, but I was actually rejecting a moment of connection and an opportunity to receive kindness and affirm my value.

Then one day, everything changed.

I had a mentor who noticed this pattern in me. After watching me deflect a compliment yet again, he gently said, "Thanh, a compliment is like a gift. When someone gives it to you, the least you can do is say 'thank you.' You don't have to explain it away – just say thank you. That's enough. When you brush off a compliment, you're essentially returning the gift unopened. It doesn't just diminish the moment, but it also sends a message to your own mind that you're not worthy of receiving good things."

I was stunned. The metaphor landed so deeply that I didn't know what to say. Growing up in an Asian family, I was always taught to be humble, polite, and respectful to others. So the idea that deflecting a compliment was like returning a gift unopened felt both foreign and uncomfortable. It was as if he had just held up a mirror and shown me something I had never seen before. felt embarrassed, realizing that by brushing off compliments, I had been ungrateful and, in a way, disrespectful to the person offering them. And, I had been turning away kindness as though I didn't deserve it.

That realization lingered in my mind. So, one Sunday afternoon, I opened the drawer again. I untied the rubber band and opened the first letter.

"Thanh's talk gave me the strength to reclaim my power as a female firefighter and future business woman."

My throat tightened. I read another.

"Anyone who feels stuck in a rut or doubts their ability to achieve something should listen to Thanh speak. She is truly inspiring."

Then another.

"Never have I listened to such a strong, inspiring, and motivating woman like Thanh. She is not only an incredible role model for everyone but especially for women. Thanh truly inspired me to take the first step, have faith, believe in myself, and invest in my growth."

Each letter felt like a mirror reflecting the light I had refused to see in myself. Tears filled my eyes as I read, and in that moment, I knew I had begun to own my story.

That was a wake-up call. That was the day I learned to say, "thank you" and accept compliments.

That tiny change felt awkward at first, but it was my first mini-shift. From that day forward, I practiced something that felt foreign but powerful: receiving compliments with gratitude. Just saying, "Thank you."

That small shift started to change how I viewed myself and helped me slowly build real, grounded confidence.

❝

*There's a big difference between humility and self-rejection. When you constantly deflect praise, you may think you're just being polite or modest, but over time, this habit reinforces a subtle but powerful message: **I don't deserve this.***

And what we repeatedly tell ourselves, we eventually believe.

Psychologists call this a form of negative self-talk. Even if it's unspoken, your mind registers your response: *Oh, this old thing* or *I was just lucky* translates internally to *I'm not really enough.* Over time, this pattern chips away at your self-worth.

But when you receive a compliment with grace, you're practicing self-acknowledgment. You're reinforcing a belief that you *are* worthy, that your efforts, character, or appearance matter and that they're seen. You are taking ownership of your accomplishments, your goodness, and your growth.

"

Confidence is not about being the loudest in the room. Confidence is about being able to stand tall, look someone in the eye, and say thank you when they recognize your light.

SUGGESTED ACTION STEPS

I share many suggested action steps with you, but please don't feel you need to do them all at once. Just pick one step that resonates with you right now and take action on it. One small step forward is far more powerful than feeling overwhelmed and doing nothing.

1. The Open the Gift Exercise

So how do you start accepting compliments, especially if it feels awkward or unnatural?

Step 1: Resist the urge to deflect.

When someone says something kind, notice your first instinct. Is it to minimize? Dismiss? Joke?

Step 2: Pause, smile, and simply say thank you.

That's it. No explanation needed. No justification.

Just: "Thank you."

You can even add, "I appreciate that," or "That means a lot coming from you." But the most important part is allowing the compliment to *land*.

This might feel uncomfortable at first, especially if you're used to pushing away praise. But like any new habit, it gets easier with practice.

What's amazing is how this small shift creates a ripple effect:

- You start hearing yourself say positive things out loud.
- You begin to internalize the idea that you *do* bring value.
- You show others how to treat you with kindness and respect.
- And you slowly build the confidence that doesn't need to shout, but simply *receives*.

2. The Mirror Exercise

This exercise might feel a little silly at first but it's powerful.

Step 1:

Stand in front of a mirror. Look into your own eyes for five minutes.

Say something kind to yourself as you would say to a friend or someone you love.

Example:

{Your name}, you showed up to class today even though you were tired. Your commitment is unwavering.

Or:

{Your name}, I'm proud of how you handled that tough conversation with grace and honesty.

It doesn't have to be dramatic. It just has to be *true*.

Step 2:

After you say the kind statement, pause. Take a breath.

Look at yourself in the mirror and say: "Thank you." That's it – just those two words. But say them with meaning.

Why does this matter? Because we often talk to ourselves more harshly than we would ever talk to anyone else. This exercise reverses that. It helps you:

- Acknowledge your effort
- Practice self-kindness
- Build internal trust
- Learn to accept compliments even from yourself

The more you practice this, the more natural it becomes to receive compliments from others without guilt or discomfort.

FINAL THOUGHTS

Learning to accept compliments might seem like a small step, but it's one of the foundational habits of confidence. Simply say "thank you," when someone compliments you. And begin the journey of building confidence so you can create the life you want and make an impact in your world.

What one small step do you commit to take to grow your confidence?

MINI-SHIFT #2:

Anchor Yourself in What Matters

"It's not hard to make decisions when you know what your values are."

– Roy E. Disney

True confidence isn't loud. It comes from knowing who you are, what you stand for, and living in alignment with it.

So much of what we're taught about building confidence is about looking outside of ourselves:

- Faking it until you make it
- Dressing or acting a certain way mainly to impress others
- Trying to outshine or prove yourself in competition
- Repeating positive affirmations (without addressing underlying beliefs)

There's nothing wrong with these practices, and they can be helpful. But there's a limit.

You can say "I'm amazing" a hundred times and still feel hollow inside. You can earn all the accolades in the world and still doubt your worth. You can be the loudest voice in the room and still feel like an imposter.

"

That's because lasting confidence doesn't come from noise. It comes from knowing yourself and standing firmly in that knowing, even when the world trembles around you.

History is full of examples of people who didn't fit our modern image of *confident* like loud, charismatic, assertive, yet changed the world through unwavering inner strength.

When Mahatma Gandhi began his 240-mile march to the Arabian Sea, there were no microphones, no shouts of protest, no fanfare. Just the soft rhythm of bare feet against dusty earth.

He was a small man in simple white cloth, walking beneath the blazing Indian sun. Villagers peeked out from their homes, watching in quiet wonder as he passed. One by one, they joined him from farmers to students, and mothers carrying children on their hips until the silent line stretched for miles.

Gandhi didn't wave a flag or raise his voice. His strength was quieter, deeper. Each step was a declaration that dignity could not be ruled by force. By the time he reached the sea and bent down to lift a handful of salt, the world was watching. That simple gesture spoke louder than any speech ever could.

That's the confidence I'm talking about. The kind that doesn't demand attention but draws it naturally. The kind that doesn't roar but radiates. It's what happens when your values, words, and actions all move in the same direction.

Mahatma Gandhi was physically frail and often soft-spoken, but his clarity of values such as nonviolence, truth, and justice, allowed him to lead a movement that freed an entire nation. His power didn't lie in outward dominance, but in his values and moral conviction. And from that foundation, he made bold moves that shaped history.

The Root of Real Confidence

Real, unshakable confidence isn't about hype. It's about *alignment*. It comes from a deep understanding of who you are and what you stand for, defined by your **core values.**

For some, that might be **integrity**, doing the right thing even when no one's watching. For others, it's **love**, leading with compassion and care. It could be **courage**, choosing growth over comfort. **Faith,** trusting that there's meaning even when you can't see the outcome.

Or **positivity,** finding light in the darkest season.

These values act as your internal compass. They guide your choices, protect your energy, and help you stand tall, even when the world feels uncertain. When you live in alignment with your values, you feel grounded. And that grounding becomes your foundation for true confidence. Without this foundation, external confidence is like a house built on sand. It crumbles under pressure.

But when your actions reflect your deepest beliefs, something shifts. You don't need applause. You don't need to convince yourself. You just know who you are. And that knowing? That's where real confidence begins.

❝

Our values are like the roots of a tree. You can't always see them, but they hold everything up. When storms come, it's not the branches or leaves that keep the tree standing; it's the roots. The deeper the roots, the steadier the tree. Your values are the roots that keep you standing when the storm hits.

A Personal Story

For a long time, I thought confidence came from performance. If I worked hard, earned awards, and succeeded in my career, I'd feel secure. So I kept striving. And yes, I achieved a lot.

But the truth?

Even with all that success, I often felt unsettled, like something was missing. It wasn't until life brought me to a moment when my titles didn't matter and the applause was gone that I was forced to ask a more honest question: <u>Who am I... without all the achievements?</u>

That question changed everything.

In 2023, due to a corporate downsizing, I separated from my role as a vice president of engineering, though just days before, I was praised as an exceptional leader who had built and led high-performing teams. My team respected and loved me. and I felt the same about them. Every morning, I woke up with a sense of purpose – there were people to support, decisions to make, problems to solve, and progress to drive. I was needed. I mattered.

Then, in an instant, it was gone. No more urgent emails. No more morning huddles. No more team counting on me. No more "Vice President" next to my name.

The next day, I sat in the silence, and it felt like the ground had opened beneath me.

I had built so much of my identity around being productive, helpful, and successful. But now I had to sit with a version of myself who had none of those things to offer. And that was terrifying.

But it was also a turning point.

Because it's often in times of deep uncertainty, in the vast space of the unknown, that we are invited to go deeper. To shed the layers of who we thought we had to be. To get curious about who we really are underneath the roles, the recognition, the routine.

It's in that quiet, uncomfortable space that reinvention begins. And that's when I began to see a different pattern.

I had a chat with a kindred soul, and we marveled at a simple truth: **chaos often comes right before something beautiful is born.** Think about it: in chemistry, before a stable compound is formed, there's often a flurry of reactions, heat, motion, energy, chaos in motion. But out of that chaos comes transformation. A new creation.

The same happens in nature. When a caterpillar enters its cocoon, it doesn't simply grow wings overnight. It dissolves, literally, into a formless liquid. Everything it once was must break down before it can become what it's meant to be. That in-between stage isn't pretty. It's dark, still, and uncertain. But inside that cocoon, transformation is quietly at work.

That's the essence of transformation, letting go of who we were to make space for who we're becoming, as Albert Einstein said, "I must be willing to give up what I am in order to become what I will be."

The same is true in business. In the weeks leading to a product launch, everything can feel messy. Deadlines collide, and teams juggle testing, feedback, approvals, unexpected bugs, last-minute changes. It's stressful. It's uncertain. It's…chaos.

But then, launch day comes. And just like that, something new exists in the world. A new product. A new solution. A new beginning.

The same pattern shows up in so many parts of life from construction projects to creative breakthroughs, even childbirth, or the big bang that creates our universe.

The middle is messy. It's uncomfortable. But it's also necessary. No mess, no progress. No chaos, no creation.

So if you ever find yourself in the thick of the unknown when the structure has fallen away, when you don't know who you are without the title, the schedule, the applause, take heart.

You might just be standing on the edge of something sacred.

Don't run from the mess – *move through it*.

Because some of the most beautiful things begin after everything falls apart.

And maybe, just maybe, confidence doesn't come from how much we do, but from how fully we know and accept who we are, especially when there's nothing left to prove.

During the days that followed the layoff, I began reflecting deeply. I wrote. I listened. I remembered moments when I felt most alive, most proud, most in flow. Through that journey, I was reminded of the five core values that I had for myself: **Love. Courage. Positivity. Humility. Perseverance.**

These weren't just nice words. They were my truth:

- **Love** is how I lead and connect, with care, compassion, and intention.
- **Courage** is not the absence of fear, but the decision to do what is right despite being afraid.
- **Positivity** is reflected in how I embrace the beauty of life and the abundance of blessings around me, striving to see the positive side of things to achieve success.
- **Humility** reminds me I don't need to have all the answers, and I just need to keep showing up with a teachable heart.

- **Perseverance** is the quiet strength that carries me through setbacks and getting me back up again and again after each failure. Similar to how the gentle flow of water creates the awe-inspiring Grand Canyon, with perseverance, individuals can attain great success.

Once I defined these values, something powerful happened: I stopped trying to prove my worth. I started living from it.

With each passing month, I began to rebuild, not from my résumé, but from my core values. Every time self-doubt crept in, I returned to my values like a compass pointing me home. When fear whispered you're not enough, courage reminded me that I've faced harder things before. When my mind raced with uncertainty, positivity invited me to look for lessons instead of losses. When my ego wanted to rush back into busyness just to feel important again, humility helped me slow down and listen. And when progress felt painfully slow, perseverance carried me through. But above all, it was love that truly healed me.

A few months later, I went to a private retreat with Jack Canfield, the author of *The Success Principles* and *Chicken Soup for the Soul*. During one of our sessions, Jack looked at me and said something that I'll never forget: "Thanh, you need to learn to love yourself. That's the highest achievement of all."

His words sank deep. I had spent decades striving to earn love through effort, helping, achieving, performing, doing. But for the first time, I realized love wasn't something to earn; it was something to embrace.

So I started practicing it, not in grand gestures, but in small, quiet ways. Allowing myself to rest without guilt. Speaking to myself with kindness. Celebrating progress instead of perfection. I began treating myself with the same compassion I so easily gave to others.

And something shifted. The more I loved myself, the more grounded and peaceful I became. I no longer needed a title to feel worthy or an achievement to feel proud. Love became the soil where all the other values — courage, positivity, humility, and perseverance — could grow strong roots.

"

Confidence, I realized, isn't about proving anything. It's about becoming everything you already are, once you finally remember to live according to your values.

Why Knowing Your Values Builds Confidence

When you don't know your values, you drift. You may say yes when you mean no. Or chasing things that don't fulfill you. Comparing yourself to others and wondering if you measure up. But when you know what you stand for, you start living with clarity, and confidence grows in that clarity. Knowing your values helps you:

- Make decisions with peace, not pressure
- Set boundaries that protect your energy
- Let go of what doesn't align, even if others don't understand
- Respect yourself, even when things don't go your way

You don't have to be the loudest. You just have to be *true*. Discovering your core values is your second mini-shift. It may feel simple, even subtle, but it changes everything. When you know your values, you stop being swayed by trends, applause, or other people's expectations. Instead, you stand on a steady foundation.

The essence of this shift is simple: **alignment breeds confidence**. When your actions and choices reflect your values, you no longer need the world's permission to stand tall. You already know who you are.

SUGGESTED ACTION STEPS

I share many suggested action steps with you, but please don't feel you need to do them all at once. Just pick one step that resonates with you right now and take action on it. One small step forward is far more powerful than feeling overwhelmed and doing nothing.

Define Your Core Values

Here's how to get started:

- Review the list of values in the Appendix A.
- Circle or highlight words that resonate.
- Narrow it down to your **top five.**

If it is difficult to narrow down to the top five, take some time to journal and reflect on these questions:

- When you are at your best, what values are you living out?
- Which values have helped you during your hardest moments?
- If you could pass down only five values to your children or someone you love, what would they be?

- Which values drive your biggest life decisions, not just what feels good, but what directs your actions?

Then write a short sentence defining what each means to you. Once you've defined your five, ask yourself, Am I living in alignment with these values today? If the answer is yes, even just a little, you're building confidence from the inside out.

Values Alignment Check-In

Each evening this week, ask yourself:
- *What value did I honor today?*
- *What value did I forget and how can I embody it tomorrow?*
- *How did I feel when I acted in alignment with who I am?*

This simple daily practice builds not just awareness, but integrity, which is the bedrock of true self-confidence.

FINAL THOUGHTS

Confidence isn't about puffing yourself up or pretending to have it all together.

It's about being deeply rooted in who you are. It's about waking up each day and living in alignment with your core values.

Your confidence doesn't come from outside praise, and it doesn't come from accomplishments. It comes from the quiet knowing that you are living your life aligned with your personal core values. Live those values boldly and your confidence will grow, because you know who you are and what you stand for in every step of the way.

What one small step do you commit to take to grow your confidence?

MINI-SHIFT #3:

Be Real, Be Free

"To be nobody but yourself in a world which is doing its best, night and day, to make you everybody else—means to fight the hardest battle which any human being can fight; and never stop fighting."

- E. E. Cummings

"You smile too much to be taken seriously as an engineer."
Someone told me that once. It wasn't the first time I had been labeled. Too soft. Too small. Too emotional. Too different. Too much of one thing, and not enough of another.

Like many professional women, especially those of us in male-dominated fields, I was constantly trying to calibrate myself: Don't be too cheerful. Don't be too bold. Don't take up too much space. Don't stand out.

So, I changed. I wore muted colors. I smiled less. I tried to fit in. I worked hard to become a version of myself that would be accepted. Palatable. Professional.

And honestly, it did not work. No matter how much I tried to fit in, I couldn't. People can sense when you are performing instead of showing up as yourself. And it was also exhausting.

Every small choice that went against who I was chipped away at my energy, my joy, and eventually, my confidence.

One day, when my daughter was just three years old, she walked into my closet with wide, curious eyes. She looked around and asked, *"Mom, you like color. Why don't you have any colorful clothes?"*

That innocent question cracked something open in me. In that moment, I realized I wasn't just dimming my light; I was also unconsciously teaching my daughter to shrink herself, to mute her own joy and authenticity, just to fit in.

And that went against everything I wanted for her. I wanted her to be bold, expressive, joyful, and free. But how could I expect her to embrace who she was if I was afraid to do the same?

"

My daughter's question reminded me that dimming my light teaches others to do the same.

That day, I made a decision to stop hiding and stop shrinking. I would start showing up fully, joyfully, unapologetically as me. That was my shift. Not dramatic. Not loud. Just a decision to stop muting myself.

I brought color back into my wardrobe. I let my smile shine. I joined Toastmaster to learn how to communicate better. I spoke up more. I intentionally looked for friends, allies, advocates and sponsors at work. I led with warmth and authenticity.

At first, people were surprised. Some looked at me oddly, unsure what to make of this new version of me. I could feel their silent question: What changed? But I kept showing up, authentically, consistently, unapologetically.

And something beautiful happened. Over time, most people began to embrace it. They welcomed me—the real me—and even appreciated the uniqueness I offered.

"

The more I showed up as myself, the more confident I became. Not because everyone accepted me, but because I accepted me.

We are conditioned from an early age to fit in, to smooth our edges. To follow the rules. But **fitting in differs from belonging.**

Fitting in means you change who you are to be accepted. *Belonging* means you are accepted because of who you are. Trying to be someone else might win you approval, but it comes at a cost that is your energy, your authenticity, and eventually, your self-confidence. Because deep down, you know you're not being you. And when you don't trust yourself to be you, how can you expect confidence to grow?

Being Authentic

This isn't just my story; it's a common human experience.

Academy Award–winning actress Viola Davis, once said, *"I lost myself for a while trying to be what I thought people wanted me to be. Then I realized, my authenticity is my superpower."*

Lady Gaga has spoken openly about how early fame pressured her to fit an image, until she chose to return to her true voice: *"Don't you ever let a soul in the world tell you that you can't be exactly who you are."*

Even Steve Jobs said, *"Your time is limited, so don't waste it living someone else's life."*

❝

Authenticity isn't just a good idea. Authenticity is a foundation for confidence and leadership.

When you show up as yourself:

- You stop performing and start connecting.
- You build deeper trust with yourself and others.
- You attract the right opportunities, relationships, and teams.
- You become someone whom others feel safe around, because your presence gives them permission to be real too.

Your smile. Your warmth. Your story. Your voice. Your experience. These are your edge and what only you can bring to the world. And when you embrace them, you unlock a level of confidence that doesn't depend on applause or approval.

Stop trying to fit into someone else's mold. Your power is in being you.

SUGGESTED ACTION STEPS

I share many suggested action steps with you, but please don't feel you need to do them all at once. Just pick one step that resonates with you right now and take action on it. One small step forward is far more powerful than feeling overwhelmed and doing nothing.

Ask yourself these questions:

- *In what areas of my life am I holding back part of who I am?*
- *What do I really want to wear, say, or create, but have hesitated to out of fear?*
- *Who would I be if I trusted that who I am is enough?*

Now, take one small step to align your outer world with your inner truth. It might be:

- Wearing something that reflects your style and spirit
- Sharing a story or opinion that reflects your values
- Smiling, even if someone once said you shouldn't

Each time you act in alignment with who you are, you grow stronger.

What Are You Hiding?

Stand in front of the mirror and say to yourself, *"I am not too much. I am not too little. I am exactly who I need to be."*

Repeat it each day this week and notice how your energy shifts when you choose to believe it.

Then, write down:

- One part of yourself you used to hide
- One reason you're proud of that part now
- One way you will show it more this week

FINAL THOUGHTS

For a long time, I thought success meant fitting in. Now I know true success begins when you stop pretending and start showing up as yourself. You were never meant to be someone else. The world needs the full version of you, not the filtered, muted, edited one.

So wear the color. Tell the story. Take up space. Smile big. Lead with your light. Because the moment you stop trying to be someone else, you free up so much energy, creativity, mental and emotional space to unlock your true potential.

Authenticity isn't a makeover; it's a mini-shift, a choice to step out from behind the curtain and let the world see the light that was always yours.

What one small step do you commit to take to grow your confidence?

MINI-SHIFT #4:

Clarity Creates Courage

"Your time is limited, so don't waste it living someone else's life. Don't be trapped by dogma – which is living with the results of other people's thinking. Don't let the noise of others' opinions drown out your own inner voice."

– Steve Jobs

It was early morning, sunlight spilling gently through the blinds of our home office. My husband walked in, expecting to see me focused, maybe taking notes or solving equations.

Instead, he froze.

On the screen was an electrical engineering lecture.

And on my face — tears. Silent, steady, unstoppable.

He rushed over, startled.

"What happened?" he asked softly.

I looked up, my voice barely above a whisper.

"I don't like this," I said.

At first, he seemed confused. "What don't you like?"

"This. This lecture. This class. This degree," I replied.

"Then… why are you doing it?" he puzzled.

I paused, feeling the weight of my own words before they even left my lips.

"Because my dad told me to."

In that moment, the truth hit me harder than I expected. I was a grown woman — married, already a mom — yet still living a script written by someone else. For years, I had been doing what I thought I should do, not what I truly wanted to do. I had followed directions for so long that I never stopped to ask myself what I really wanted or even realized that I had a choice.

I was working toward a PhD in Electrical Engineering, a prestigious path on paper, but one that didn't feel like mine.

That morning, as my husband stood there and I wiped the tears from my cheeks, something inside me shifted.

For the first time, I realized: I had a choice.

And that simple awareness, that I could choose differently, became the first spark of transformation.

> **"**
>
> *Confidence grows when we stop living by default and start living by design. And that begins with one bold question:*
> **What do I really want?**

There's a joke in many Asian families that a child has three career options: they can become a doctor, an engineer, or a disappointment. I used to laugh at that joke, until I realized how deeply it reflected my upbringing. From the moment I was born, I was handed not just a name, but a plan: what to study, who to be friends with, which career to pursue, and later on, even who to marry. It wasn't out of cruelty; it was love wrapped in fear — fear that I wouldn't be safe if I didn't follow the *successful path*. But it left little room for me to explore my own desires.

And it's not just me. Across cultures, many people grow up with layers of "shoulds" and "should nots." We're told what a good life looks like, and what success, happiness, or fulfillment are supposed to mean. And somewhere along the way, we lose our voice. We know how to meet expectations, but we forget how to listen to our hearts.

There's a scene in the movie *Runaway Bride* that captures this perfectly. Julia Roberts' character keeps getting engaged, but she always runs away at the altar. One day, her new love interest notices she always says her favorite eggs are the same as whoever she's dating. It's scrambled with one man, poached with another, over-easy with the next. She doesn't even know how she likes her own eggs.

That was me. That might be you.

"

So many of us are living our lives like we're ordering someone else's breakfast. And that confusion chips away at our confidence. Because when you don't know what you want, you become easily swayed. You look for answers outside yourself. You stay in the wrong job, relationship, or life path too long because you haven't given yourself permission to want something different.

Confidence isn't possible when you don't know what you want. It's like running hard in the wrong direction.

This chapter is about a mini-shift that's subtle but life-changing: shifting from living by "shoulds" to living by choice. Not a giant leap — just the decision to pause and ask, *What do I really want here?*

Choose Your Motivation

Think of it like driving: you can be the most skilled driver in the world, but if you're in the wrong lane, you'll never arrive where you need to go. The mini-shift is turning the wheel toward your own lane. Once you do, even small moves keep you on course.

"

When you know what you want, you stop apologizing for it. You stop explaining yourself. You start walking your own path instead of borrowing someone else's.

But there's good news. Clarity is a skill.

And it starts with asking questions and listening for your own answers. When you know what you want, you move through life with more confidence and less comparison.

Psychologists call it **autonomous motivation** – doing something because it aligns with your values and desires, not because someone else told you to. Research from Deci and Ryan's Self-Determination Theory (1985) shows that people who live in alignment with what they want experience greater happiness, energy, and purpose.

Contrast that with **introjected motivation**, which is when you act out of guilt, pressure, or to meet someone else's standard. Over time, this leads to burnout, resentment, and a hollow success. You might look like you have it all, but inside, you feel like something is missing.

Gallup's 2023 report revealed that nearly 70% of workers are disengaged at work. And it's not just because of poor management. It's often because they're in roles that don't align with what they want.

Many people wake up every morning and go through the motions, showing up, performing tasks, meeting expectations, but feeling empty inside. They've climbed ladders only to realize they were leaning against the wrong wall. They stay in their jobs because it's comfortable, familiar, or because someone once told them it was the "right" path.

Disengagement isn't just about work performance; it's about identity. When what we do no longer reflects who we are, a quiet disconnection begins between our head and our heart, our effort and our energy. Over time, that gap grows into burnout, frustration, or a sense of being lost.

Another study from Roese and Summerville (2005) found that nearly half of people regret major life decisions – from career to relationships – because they didn't stop to ask, *Is this what I truly want?*

When we know what we want:

- We stop chasing trends.
- We stop comparing ourselves to others.
- We start living from the inside out.

And that is the beginning of real, grounded confidence.

SUGGESTED ACTION STEPS

I share many suggested action steps with you, but please don't feel you need to do them all at once. Just pick one step that resonates with you right now and take action on it. One small step forward is far more powerful than feeling overwhelmed and doing nothing.

Ask Better Questions

So how do you begin the journey of discovering what you want, especially if you've spent a lifetime chasing someone else's definition of success? Start with these three steps:

When you're unsure, don't stop at "I don't know."

Ask yourself:

- *What do I want right now?*
- *If I did know what I want, what might it be?*
- *What would I do if I wasn't afraid?*

This second question helps bypass mental blocks. The brain doesn't like unanswered questions, so it will search for possibilities. Over time, this practice rewires your brain to tune in to your own voice.

Create a "101 Wants" List

This exercise isn't about materialism, and it will help you gain clarity.

Write down 101 things you want. Big or small. (*I want to take a road trip alone. I want to feel peace when I wake up. I want to try a pottery class.*)

Let it be messy and incomplete. The goal is to unlock your voice again.

FINAL THOUGHTS

Knowing what you want isn't selfish. It's self-aware. When you know what you want, you stop shrinking to fit into someone else's version of life. You stop apologizing for dreaming bigger, choosing differently, or saying no. You begin living on purpose, not just out of habit. And with each honest choice, you build confidence. So today, ask the question, *What do I want?*

And then listen for the answer. That answer is the beginning of your becoming.

Knowing what you want doesn't mean having your whole future figured out. It means making one clear choice today that reflects your truth, not someone else's. That's the mini-shift, and it's enough to change your direction entirely.

What one small step do you commit to take to grow your confidence?

MINI-SHIFT #5:

Let Your Why Lead You

"Courage is not the absence of fear, but rather the judgment that something else is more important than fear."

- Ambrose Redmoon

When you know why you're doing something, you find the courage to act, even when fear is loud.

You may remember the story I shared in the previous chapter about my daughter asking why I no longer wore colorful clothes. That simple, innocent question made me realize how much of myself I had muted out of fear of judgment. Reclaiming my vibrant colors wasn't just about clothing, it was about daring to be fully authentic again.

When I reflect on that moment now, I see it as more than a lesson in authenticity. It also revealed my *why*. If I don't dare to be myself, how can I teach my daughter to be herself? If I kept hiding or shrinking for approval, what message would I be sending her?

My *why* isn't just about me. It's about the kind of mother I want to be, the legacy I want to leave, and the future I hope she grows into. That deeper purpose gave me the courage to make the change, even when it felt scary at first.

So, I made a decision. Even if it was scary…I would be me. Colorful clothes. Loud laugh. Heart-centered leadership. Because my *why* was bigger than my fear.

Let's talk about what a *why* really is. Your *why* is your reason. Your purpose. Your fuel.

It's the thing that drives you, even when things get hard. It's what makes effort feel meaningful and setbacks feel survivable. Viktor Frankl, a Holocaust survivor and psychiatrist, wrote, *"Those who have a 'why' to live can bear almost any 'how.'"*

In his book, *Man's Search for Meaning*, Frankl observed that people who survived unthinkable suffering weren't necessarily the strongest or the smartest; they were the ones with something to live for, someone they loved, something they dreamed of, a reason that transcended the pain.

That principle is just as true in everyday life. Why do some people show up to physical therapy week after week, even in pain? Because they want to walk their daughter down the aisle.

Why do people face their fear of public speaking? *Because they believe their message can change lives.*

Why does a parent run into danger to protect their child, even if they're afraid? *Because their love is stronger than their fear.*

Your *why* might be quiet. It doesn't have to be dramatic, but it must be true.

When you know your *why*:

- You stop second-guessing yourself.
- You stop chasing every trend or every bit of approval.
- You start showing up with purpose.

A powerful study published in *Psychological Science* by researchers Patrick Hill and Nicholas Turiano (2014) examined data from over 6,000 adults in the Midlife in the United States (MIDUS) study. The researchers found something remarkable: people with a strong sense of purpose not only handled stress better and experienced greater psychological resilience – they also lived longer. Having a clear sense of purpose was associated with a 15% reduction in the risk of death, regardless of the person's age, gender, emotional well-being, or physical health. Purpose was a protective factor across all stages of adulthood. Purpose doesn't just make us emotionally stronger; and it makes us physically stronger too.

Another study from Stanford University with over 1,600 high school and college students found that students who connected their academic goals to a deeper personal reason (like helping their family or giving back to their community) were more likely to persevere, improve grades, and feel more fulfilled (Yeager et al., 2014).

What does this mean for confidence?

Both the Hill & Turiano (2014) and the Yeager et al. (2014) studies show that when people connect to a deeper sense of purpose, they experience greater resilience, more motivation, increased follow-through, and better mental and emotional well-being. These are building blocks of true confidence.

"

Confidence isn't just believing you can do something;
it's trusting that what you're doing matters.

When you have a clear *why,* your confidence doesn't depend on external validation. Instead, it comes from within, from the conviction that your actions are aligned with your values and purpose.

In both studies, purpose helped people push through difficult, uncertain, or uncomfortable situations, whether it was boring or challenging schoolwork (Yeager et al.), or the stressors of adult life and mortality (Hill & Turiano).

Self-doubt thrives in uncertainty. But when you're anchored by your purpose, you're less likely to be shaken by fear. You're more willing to act even if you feel unsure. This is exactly what confidence looks like in real life.

A Personal Story

I grew up in post-war Vietnam, when it was still a third-world country. The war had destroyed much of the critical infrastructure. We were poor and often without electricity or running water, and sometimes without food.

When I was sixteen, my uncle from America offered to sponsor me to study in the U.S. It felt like a dream come true. It was an opportunity that could transform my life and my family's future. I was thrilled to land in America, a place filled with cars, skyscrapers, and people who looked so different from me. I thought, *Yay! I made it to the land of opportunity.*

But within a few weeks, that dream turned into a nightmare. My uncle, the one who had promised to help me, sexually abused me and kicked me out of his house. I was sixteen, in a foreign country, unable to speak English, and with no money. My dream was shattered.

I found a job at a small Vietnamese coffee shop, earning much less than minimum wage because it was the only place that would hire me. I studied during the day, worked at night, and wore a headset to listen to the radio even while sleeping to learn English. For months, I cried myself to sleep every night; but even through the tears, I kept pushing forward.

People sometimes ask me now, "How did you have the courage to move across continents as a teenager and stay after everything you went through? How did you find the confidence to keep going?"

I didn't have courage or confidence.

What I *did* have was a powerful *why*.

My *why* was my family. I wanted to make them proud. I wanted to build a better future for myself and my family. I wanted to turn pain into purpose. And that *why* became my anchor — the quiet force that kept me moving forward even when I was shaking inside.

Each time I took one trembling step, it built a tiny bit of strength.

> **"**
>
> *Each time I faced fear and kept going, I built the muscle of confidence.*

And over time, step by shaky step, that muscle grew stronger.

Confidence is something we *build* by remembering our *why*, especially when everything feels uncertain.

> **"**
>
> *Think of your **why** like a lighthouse. It doesn't calm the storm, but it helps you find your way through it.*

The storms will come. The waves will rise. But your *why* cuts through the fog and points you back to your true direction. Even when you feel small, even when you doubt yourself, that steady light keeps you moving forward.

This is the mini-shift: moving from drifting without direction to being guided by purpose. It doesn't mean you'll have everything figured out, but it means you'll know why you're choosing the next step, and that makes all the difference.

SUGGESTED ACTION STEPS

I share many suggested action steps with you, but please don't feel you need to do them all at once. Just pick one step that resonates with you right now and take action on it. One small step forward is far more powerful than feeling overwhelmed and doing nothing.

If you're feeling lost, uncertain, or held back by fear. It's time to reconnect with your *why*.

Here are three steps to help:

1. Look Back at a Time You Were Brave

Think of when you did something that scared you. Maybe you applied for a new job. Maybe you told someone how you really felt. Maybe you stood up for yourself for the first time.

Ask yourself, *What fear did I overcome? What gave me the strength to do it anyway?*

Chances are, a strong *why* was behind that courage.

2. Ask Deep Questions

Use journaling or quiet reflection to explore:

- *What matters most to me in life?*
- *Who or what am I willing to struggle for?*
- *What impact do I want to leave behind?*
- *What do I believe in so strongly that I'd speak up for it, even if it made me uncomfortable?*

3. Turn It into a Statement

Use this simple template to write your *why*: *I want to* _____ *so that* _____ .

Examples:

I want to lead with honesty so others feel safe to do the same. I want to grow my business so I can create generational wealth for my family. I want to write this book so that my story can help someone else heal.

Post it somewhere visible. Let it guide your decisions, your actions, and your mindset.

FINAL THOUGHTS

We often think confidence comes from feeling fearless. But more often, it comes from being **purpose-driven**. When your *why* is clear, you don't have to wait until you feel ready.

You just begin, because the reason is too important not to. So today, ask yourself:

What matters enough that I'd do it afraid? What truth is worth showing up for even when it's uncomfortable? That's your *why*. Let it carry you through the fear, through the noise, and through the doubt.

Because confidence isn't the absence of fear; it's the presence of purpose. And the moment you discover your *why*, you'll discover your courage too. Discovering your *why* is the mini-shift that transforms every action into purpose; and purpose is where lasting confidence begins.

What one small step do you commit to take to grow your confidence?

MINI-SHIFT #6:

Move First, Confidence Follows

"Inaction breeds doubt and fear. Action breeds confidence and courage. If you want to conquer fear, do not sit home and think about it. Go out and get busy."

– Dale Carnegie

How do you get over fear, imposter syndrome, or those nagging negative thoughts?

I've never learned how to silence those voices. They whisper familiar doubts every time I'm about to step into something new:

- *You're not good enough.*
- *People will laugh at you.*
- *You'll embarrass yourself.*
- *You have no idea what you're doing.*

But here's the shift: I act anyway.

I don't wait for the fear to go away.

I don't try to eliminate all doubt before I begin.

Instead, I've learned to move forward with the voices still present. And, as I took actions, I built confidence.

The best way to build real confidence is through action. **Action comes first. Confidence follows.**

And no story captures this truth better than that of Phil Knight, the founder of Nike.

When Phil was twenty-four, he had what he called a crazy idea. He loved running, not just the competition, but the clarity and freedom it gave him. He dreamed of creating better shoes so others could experience that same joy. But he had no business, no connections, and no plan. Just an idea and a heart full of uncertainty.

One day, he decided to act. He bought a plane ticket to Japan because he had studied how Japanese products disrupted industries, and he wanted to explore Japanese shoes. He had never visited the country before and didn't speak a word of Japanese.

Standing on the streets of Kobe, the air thick with salt and humidity, his heart pounded harder than his footsteps. Half a world away from home, he was chasing a dream no one else could see. He had no plan, no appointment, and no idea where to start, except the belief that if he showed up, something might happen.

One morning, over casual conversation, a traveling salesman mentioned a small company in town called Onitsuka Tiger. Acting on instinct, he found the address and went there.

He walked into their office uninvited, trying to look more confident than he felt. Moments later, he was sitting across from a table of executives in pressed suits who spoke little English. His palms were damp. His mind was racing. Then came the question:

"Who do you represent, Mr. Knight?"

Phil hesitated, his stomach twisting. And then, before his fear could stop him, he said,

"Blue Ribbon Sports."

There was no Blue Ribbon Sports. Not yet.

But that moment of spontaneous courage changed everything. He pitched importing their shoes to America, and to his surprise, they agreed to send samples.

When he got back home, he asked his parents for a small loan to place his first order. He began selling shoes out of the trunk of his car. That single, uncertain step, taken in a haze of doubt and adrenaline, became the first step toward Nike, a brand that later defined movement itself.

And decades later, Nike's slogan would perfectly capture the essence of that day:

Just Do It.

Phil's story reminds us that confidence doesn't come before action.

He didn't wait to feel ready. He acted, and confidence followed.

❝

*We often believe that confidence must come before action, and that we have to **feel** ready before we start. But the truth, supported by psychology and real-life experience, is that **confidence is a result of action, not its prerequisite.***

Decades ago, Stanford psychologist Albert Bandura introduced the concept of **self-efficacy,** which is the belief in our ability to succeed in specific situations. His research found that one of the strongest ways to build this belief isn't through thinking or waiting until we feel prepared. It's through mastery experiences, taking action, succeeding (even in small ways), and building momentum from those successes (Bandura, 1977). Every time we take action and follow through, we prove to ourselves that we're capable. And that fuels the next step.

Harvard researchers Teresa Amabile and Steven Kramer echoed this in their groundbreaking study of over 12,000 workday diaries. They found that making even the tiniest progress in meaningful work creates what they call the progress principle. That progress, however small, boosts motivation, engagement, and yes, confidence (Amabile & Kramer, 2011).

It's not about waiting for big wins. It's about showing up, doing something meaningful, and letting that forward motion lift you.

This ties closely to the work of Dr. Timothy Pychyl from Carleton University, who studies procrastination and human motivation. He flips the common assumption that we must be motivated or confident *before* acting. His findings suggest the opposite: when we start taking action, even if it's tiny and imperfect, we begin to **feel more motivated and confident** (Pychyl, 2013). Action fuels emotion and not the other way around.

"

This "act first, confidence later" approach doesn't just apply to psychology. It's also how many of the world's most successful entrepreneurs operate.

Dr. Saras Sarasvathy's groundbreaking research at the University of Virginia found that expert entrepreneurs don't wait until they feel fully prepared or confident. Instead, they follow what she calls effectual logic. They start with what they have, take action, gather feedback, and adapt quickly. Rather than planning everything perfectly, they move forward before they feel ready, and confidence grows from doing. Success, in this mindset, isn't built on certainty. It's built on courage, curiosity, and momentum. (Sarasvathy, 2001)

And if you're someone who has struggled with self-doubt or imposter syndrome, you're not alone. Psychologists Pauline Clance and Suzanne Imes coined the term *Imposter Phenomenon* in the 1970s, and their research shows that people who push through their doubt and keep acting who continue learning and delivering results eventually begin to see themselves differently (Clance & Imes, 1978). Even people who don't feel confident can become confident through repeated action and positive reinforcement.

This aligns beautifully with Carol Dweck's work on a growth mindset. According to Dweck, people who believe that abilities can be developed (rather than being fixed) are more willing to take action despite fear or uncertainty. And every time they do, they grow confidence (Dweck, 2006).

❝

The takeaway? **Confidence isn't something you wait for; it's something you generate through action.** *Take one step. Then another. Let your progress, not perfection, be the fuel that strengthens your belief in yourself.*

That's the shift. Confidence isn't the fuel for action. Action is the fuel for confidence.

I think of it like riding a bicycle. You can't wait to push the pedals until you feel steady – balance only comes once you're moving. In the same way, clarity and confidence come through motion, not before it.

For years, I believed I needed to feel confident first. I thought confidence was a prerequisite to speaking up, applying for the opportunity, or taking the leap. But the opposite is true.

Every time I acted, even shaking, even stumbling, I discovered I was braver than I believed. And with each small step, the doubts grew quieter.

This is the mini-shift: from waiting until you feel ready to moving forward while still uncertain. The doubts don't disappear. You just stop letting them drive.

SUGGESTED ACTION STEPS

I share many suggested action steps with you, but please don't feel you need to do them all at once. Just pick one step that resonates with you right now and take action on it. One small step forward is far more powerful than feeling overwhelmed and doing nothing.

So how do you take action when fear is loud and self-doubt is heavy?

Here are three powerful shifts to help you move forward:

1. Name the Fear but Don't Let It Drive

You don't need to ignore your fear. Acknowledge it.

Say: *I hear you, fear. Thank you for trying to protect me.*

Then gently say, *But I'm choosing to act anyway.*

You can let fear ride in the car, but it doesn't get to touch the steering wheel.

2. Anchor to Your Purpose

Fear is often loudest when your focus is on yourself: *what if I fail? What will people think?*

Shift the focus. Ask yourself: *Who am I here to help? Who needs me to show up? What's the greater purpose behind this step?*

Purpose shrinks fear, and service turns nerves into fuel.

3. Take a Tiny Step

Don't try to leap the whole staircase. Just take the next step.

Send the email.

Sign up for the class.

Speak up once in the meeting.

Record a 30-second video.

Submit the application.

Courage grows through repetition. Every tiny act of bravery strengthens your belief in yourself.

And soon, you'll look back and realize you didn't "conquer" fear. You stopped letting it stop you.

The 3-Step Fear & Action Journal

Each night for the next five days, take 10 minutes to reflect on these prompts:

Step 1: Identify a Fear

What's something you felt afraid to do today or avoided doing altogether?

Example: *I wanted to ask for feedback but worried I'd seem needy.*

Step 2: Reframe with Purpose

Ask:

Why does this action matter?

Who benefits if I take it?

What value does it bring?

Example: *I want to grow. Honest feedback helps me become better and shows my team that I value their insights.*

Step 3: Commit to a Small Action

What is **one small thing** you can do today related to that fear?

Example: *"I am sending a message to my mentor asking for one thing I could improve.*

By the end of the week, you'll have five fears, five reframes, and five steps taken no matter how small. That is the foundation of confidence.

FINAL THOUGHTS

You don't have to wait until you feel fearless to take action. You just need to be willing to move with fear, not against it. The lotus blooms from the mud, and courage grows through discomfort.

You may have doubts and still show up boldly. So the next time fear whispers that you're not ready, look it in the eye and say, *Maybe not. But I'm doing it anyway.* And every time you do, you become a little more confident, a little more grounded, and a lot more unstoppable. So today, take the next step. Let action lead. And let confidence follow.

What one small step do you commit to take to grow your confidence?

MINI-SHIFT #7:

Change the Story, Change Your Life

"We suffer more often in imagination than in reality."

- Seneca

Have you ever noticed how the mind has a way of turning small storms into full-blown hurricanes? A single comment. A missed email. A quiet room. Suddenly, you're spiraling into a storyline of worst-case scenarios.

"They're ignoring me. Or I must have done something wrong. This is going to ruin everything."

That's the mind at work; specifically, the part of our mind that dwells, exaggerates, and ruminates.

Seneca's words hit especially close to home for me during a season of uncertainty. My husband had been furloughed, and we were both searching for jobs. I was offered a role but I turned it down because it didn't feel like the right fit. Still, the decision was heavy. What if I had made the wrong choice? What if nothing else came along?

One day, my daughter overheard me talking about it and asked, "But Mom…is there anything else out there? You said the job market is so bad."

In her voice, I heard my own fear reflected back to me. But instead of feeding that fear, I paused. I breathed. And I chose to reframe.

I told her, "A few decades ago, we didn't have automobiles. Now it's an industry employing millions. The same is true for air travel, renewable energy, and artificial intelligence. The world is always expanding. Opportunities are always being created. As long as we don't give up or lose heart, we'll find something great."

66

The storm wasn't outside; it was in my thoughts. And
I chose not to let it grow.

That moment reminded me of a powerful truth: we can't always control what happens to us. But we can choose how we respond to our thoughts *about* what's happening.

Viktor Frankl, the Holocaust survivor and psychiatrist, once wrote, "Between stimulus and response, there is a space. In that space is our power to choose our response. In our response lies our growth and our freedom."

That quote beautifully captures the heart of this mini-shift. Confidence isn't about controlling every situation but about recognizing that space, the pause between what happens and how we choose to think about it.

When my son was five years old, he once looked at me during a time-out and said, "Mom, I'm sitting still on the outside, but I'm jumping up and down in my mind." I tried to look serious but couldn't help smiling on the inside.

66

Even at five, he understood something profound:
while we can't always control our circumstances, we
can always choose what happens in our minds.

Confidence begins in the space where awareness meets choice.

So much of our suffering doesn't come from reality but rather from our thoughts about reality. It comes from the voice in our head that whispers, *"You're not enough. You'll fail. Everyone's doing better than you. You're falling behind. This will never change."*

Unchecked, these thoughts become mental habits, and those habits shape how we feel, how we act, and who we believe ourselves to be.

We think a lot. Researchers estimate that the average person's mind generates thousands of thoughts each day. Most are habitual, and because of our brain's built-in negativity bias, we usually focus more on threats and mistakes than on what's working well (Baumeister et al., 2001; Killingsworth & Gilbert, 2010; Watkins, 2008).

And because of what psychologists call the negativity bias, our minds usually pay more attention to what's wrong than what's right. This bias once helped us survive by noticing danger quickly, but today it often works against us, fueling worry, self-doubt, and comparison.

Studies show that repetitive negative thinking is linked to higher stress, anxiety, and depression. The more we replay the same discouraging thoughts, the more those neural pathways strengthen, making them easier to access next time. But the reverse is also true.

❝

When we intentionally choose more balanced, compassionate thoughts, we can begin to rewire the brain toward calm, confidence, and resilience.

We don't have to believe everything we think. Thoughts are patterns, not facts. And with awareness and practice, we can change them.

When we learn to notice, question, and reframe our inner dialogue, we take back control of our mental and emotional well-being. This isn't about toxic positivity, and it's not about pretending everything is great. It's about choosing the thoughts that move us forward and are grounded in truth, possibility, and compassion.

The Reframe Tool: A 4-Step Practice for Mental Freedom

Step 1: Catch the Extreme Thought

Start by becoming aware of black-and-white, all-or-nothing, or overly dramatic thoughts.

Examples:

- *I'll never get through this.*
- *This ruins everything.*
- *I always mess things up.*
- *Nobody cares.*

If it includes words like always, never, everyone, or nothing; you've likely caught one. Awareness is the first act of empowerment. You can't change a thought you don't recognize.

Step 2: Challenge Its Validity

Once you catch the thought, ask:

- *Is this absolutely true?*
- *What evidence do I have for this thought?*

- *Is there another way to look at it?*

Then stretch your perspective:

- Future Looking: *Will this matter in 10 days? 10 months? 10 years?*
- Past Looking: *Have I faced something harder? What helped me get through it?*

Also, separate facts from interpretation. We often blur the line between what happened and what we think it means.

Step 3: Correct with Evidence

Now replace the thought with something more helpful, balanced, and empowering. Ask:

- *What would I say to a friend if they were thinking this?*
- *What's a more compassionate way to see this?*
- *What's one reason to stay hopeful?*

Examples:

- *I've faced uncertainty before, and found a way through.*
- *One challenge doesn't define me.*
- *There are still possibilities I haven't explored.*
- *This setback might redirect me to something better.*

This is not about blind optimism. It's about constructive realism.

Step 4: Act – Take Steps Within Your Control

Now that you've shifted your perspective, take action. Even by doing something small.

- Move your body.
- Write down three things you're grateful for.

- Text someone who lifts you up.
- Cross one thing off your to-do list.
- Speak one kind sentence to yourself out loud.

Action is the bridge between mental clarity and emotional momentum. You don't need to fix everything right now – just do one thing that reminds you that you are not stuck. You are not powerless. You are capable of movement and choice.

"

Tell yourself a better story. **The story you believe shapes the life you lead.**

There was a moment in my engineering career when I nearly walked away, not because I wasn't capable, but because I believed someone else's story about me.

I was called into a meeting by my boss. I had no idea what it was about, but I quickly found out. He looked at me and said, *"I want you to rank yourself among your teammates."*

I was stunned. How do you even respond to that? I refused out of principle, humility, and confusion. That's when he dropped the bomb.

"You're at the bottom of the group. You're not meeting expectations."

Then came the words I'll never forget:

"You should probably throw your engineering degree away because you're not smart enough."

I had graduated from UC Berkeley with honors. I was pursuing a master's degree in engineering while working full-time. I had once studied in one of Vietnam's top schools for gifted students. I had won awards in math and science. I had worked hard for everything I had. And yet... I believed him.

In the days and weeks that followed, his voice echoed in my mind. I started questioning everything from my intelligence to my belonging to my future. I felt ashamed. I cried. I went to counseling. I told myself maybe I *didn't* belong. Maybe I had fooled everyone. Maybe I wasn't enough. I almost quit.

That boss's opinion was just one voice, but it became my inner voice – because I let it.

And that's the real danger: when we unconsciously adopt someone else's narrative, we give away our power. We let their words become our story. And once that story takes root, it shapes everything, including our emotions, our confidence, our actions.

The Stories We Tell Ourselves

Events are neutral. It's the *story* we attach to them that creates our emotional experience.

- Someone doesn't respond to your message. The story: *They're ignoring me.*
- You get tough feedback. The story: *I'm a failure.*
- A friend cancels plans. The story: *They don't really care about me.*

But what if those stories aren't true? What if there's another way to interpret the situation that is more compassionate, more grounded, and more empowering?

That's when we need to tell ourselves *better* stories – not fake ones, not sugar-coated lies – ones that lift us instead of crush us.

Psychologists call this **cognitive reappraisal**. It's a powerful tool in emotional regulation and in building lasting confidence.

Here's what that looks like in real life:

Unhelpful Story	Better Story
I must be the weakest link. I'm not smart enough.	*One person's opinion doesn't define me. I'm growing, and I belong here.*
They were rude to me — they don't respect me.	*Maybe they're struggling. But their actions don't define how I see myself.*
I'm falling behind. Everyone else is ahead.	*I'm on my own timeline. Progress isn't a race — it's a personal path.*

The Stories We Absorb from Childhood

Some of our most harmful stories started long before we entered the workplace. Maybe you were told you were too sensitive, too loud, not smart, or not pretty enough. Maybe you were praised only when you achieved, so you began believing you had to earn love and approval.

I grew up in Vietnam, where love was rarely spoken; it was shown. Parents didn't say "I love you"; they made sure you had food on the table, clean clothes to wear, and a roof over your head. Life was hard, and survival came before feelings. My mother believed, with all her heart, that education was the only way out of poverty. She watched my grades closely, checked my homework every day, and expected perfection. Getting straight A's wasn't celebrated; it was the standard.

When I didn't meet that standard, she became angry. She would yell, chase me around the house, sometimes hit me with a bamboo stick until I had bloody marks all over my body. Through tears, I would hear her say that my life would be nothing, that I didn't deserve her care because I hadn't done my job by earning good grades.

It took me many years to understand that beneath her harsh words was the fear of poverty, of a life with no way out. But as a child, I didn't know that. What I learned instead was that love must be earned, and worth must be proven. That story stayed with me for a long time, shaping how I saw myself and how hard I worked to be enough.

These early narratives are powerful. They become default settings in our brain. But here's the good news: you can rewrite the script. You can pause and say, *Is this story helping me or hurting me?* You can tell yourself something better. Something truer.

And when you do that consistently, you begin to trust yourself again. You stop relying on external validation. You start rebuilding confidence from the inside out.

Writing A New Story

After that painful meeting with my boss, where he told me to *throw my engineering degree away because I wasn't smart enough*, I was devastated because I believed his words.

Months later, something shifted.

I can't remember the exact day it happened or what sparked it. But I do remember the moment I found out he had said the same thing to my friend, another woman engineer in the company. I was mad. No, I was furious.

How funny — we are often kinder to others than we are to ourselves. That moment opened my eyes. I realized the problem wasn't me; it was the story he was trying to make us believe.

So, I stopped accepting his version of who I was —and started reclaiming my own.

- I remembered my education, my perseverance, my accomplishments.
- I leaned into my values: love, courage, positivity, humility, and perseverance.
- I stopped shrinking and started leading, first in my own life, then in those of others.

But by then, I had internalized the damage. It took months, years even, to unlearn that story, to reclaim the truth, and to realize his story wasn't mine.

People will always have opinions. Some will doubt you. Some will project their fears onto you. But you don't have to carry every word as truth. You get to decide:

What's the story I want to live by?

That's the mini-shift: catching the destructive thought in real time, then replacing it with one that serves you.

SUGGESTED ACTION STEPS

I share many suggested action steps with you, but please don't feel you need to do them all at once. Just pick one step that resonates with you right now and take action on it. One small step forward is far more powerful than feeling overwhelmed and doing nothing.

Reclaim Your Narrative

Use this exercise to identify and rewrite the unhelpful stories that may be limiting your confidence.

1. Identify the Trigger Moment

Think of a moment that made you feel small, insecure, or not good enough. *Example:* A coworker didn't acknowledge your contribution during a meeting.

2. Write Down the Story You Told Yourself

What belief did you form in that moment?

Example: *I must not matter. My ideas aren't valuable.*

3. Ask Yourself How that Story Was Serving You. And if It Didn't Serve You Well, Rewrite the Story

What's a more empowering version of the story?

Example: *My voice matters, even if others don't always notice. I can advocate for myself.*

FINAL THOUGHTS

We don't get to choose every situation life throws at us. But we *do* get to choose the meaning we assign to it. And the meaning you choose and the story you tell have the power to build or break your confidence.

So when the old voices rise up… pause. Take a breath. And tell yourself a better story. You are *not* what they said. You *are* not what happened to you. You *are* who you decide to become.

Your mind is powerful. But it is not always accurate. It's a storyteller, and sometimes, it tells stories that are heavy, scary, and untrue.

But you get to choose which stories to keep. You get to write a new narrative, one thought at a time. Confidence doesn't come from never having negative thoughts. It comes from recognizing those thoughts and choosing something better.

So, the next time your inner critic speaks up, pause. Listen. Then ask: *Is this thought helping me or hurting me?* And if it's the latter, reframe it. Rewrite it. Reclaim it.

Because you are not your thoughts. You are the *thinker* of your thoughts, and that means you have the power to shape them, steer them, and rise above them. Let that be your practice today.

What one small step do you commit to take to grow your confidence?

MINI-SHIFT #8:

Stop Comparing, Start Becoming

"Comparison is the thief of joy."

- Theodore Roosevelt

The morning sun glows golden over the starting line.

A hush falls over the field as the hare stretches his long legs, smirking at the turtle beside him. Dust rises gently under his feet while the turtle, calm and unhurried, adjusts his shell and looks straight ahead.

The whistle blows.

The hare explodes forward with a blur of motion, wind slicing past his ears, the world behind him fading into nothing. Every few leaps, he glances back and laughs. The turtle is still there, far behind, moving slowly, steadily, methodically, one step, then another, then another.

Confident in his lead, the hare slows down. The grass feels soft beneath him; the sun is warm on his fur. Plenty of time, he thinks, stretching out under a tree. The sounds of the forest lull him, a bird's call, the rustle of leaves, until his eyelids grow heavy.

Meanwhile, the turtle keeps going.

His shell catches the afternoon light. Each step presses a quiet print into the dusty path. He doesn't look back. He doesn't wonder how far the hare has gone. He moves forward, one deliberate, grounded step at a time.

By the time the hare wakes, the light has shifted. Shadows have grown long. In a panic, he sprints toward the finish line with his heart pounding, legs burning; but it's too late. The turtle is already there, steady and smiling, crossing with quiet certainty.

No rush.

No comparisons.

Just persistence.

And in the end, the turtle wins.

As a coach, I have found that one of the biggest culprits behind low confidence is the habit of comparing ourselves to others. We look at our neighbor's grass and think it's greener than ours, and then we feel bad about ours. We scroll through social media and see highlight reels of people landing dream jobs, traveling the world, getting promoted, buying homes. Our brain whispers, *You're falling behind*. We compare our journey to theirs, and instead of fueling us forward, the comparison paralyzes us.

But as the story of the turtle and the hare reminds us, comparison doesn't just hurt our self-confidence when we perceive others as being ahead; it can also hurt us when we believe we're ahead of others. When that happens, we risk becoming arrogant. We stop learning. We stop growing. We slow down—just like the hare, who was so busy measuring himself against the turtle that he forgot to keep running his own race.

Comparison is self-defeating. When we focus too much on someone else's lane, we lose sight of our own. We begin to question our worth, our timeline, and our abilities. That doubt creeps in, chipping away at our confidence. We start thinking, *Why am I not there yet?* or *Maybe I'm not good enough*. Comparison is the thief of joy and the enemy of growth.

Confidence doesn't come from being ahead of others. It comes from knowing you're moving forward in the right direction for you. Just like the turtle, it's the quiet, consistent steps, taken with purpose and without distraction, that lead to meaningful progress.

Eliud Kipchoge, who broke the two-hour barrier for the marathon (in a special event), is known for his speed and for his mindset. He often says the real race is with yourself.

Only the disciplined ones in life are free...a man becomes great by running his own race.

Kipchoge trains in rural Kenya, stays humble, and avoids media frenzy or comparison. He believes in personal mastery rather than outperforming others.

Meb Keflezighi, an American long-distance runner, was 38 years old and considered past his prime when he won the Boston Marathon in 2014, just one year after the bombing. He was not expected to win, but he trained silently and strategically.

I just focused on my own pace. I wasn't running against others. I was running for Boston.

Keflezighi's story proves that running your own race, mentally and literally, can lead to miraculous victories.

In her memoir *Becoming*, former First Lady Michelle Obama reflects on how she learned to stop comparing herself to others, especially in elite academic and professional environments. Growing up in the South Side of Chicago, she often felt like she didn't belong at Princeton or later at Harvard Law. But she realized that constantly measuring herself against others made her feel not enough.

"Your story is what you have, what you will always have. It is something to own."

This quote captures her mindset shift to embrace her own path, background, and values instead of trying to conform to someone else's version of success.

The Psychology of Comparison

In 1954, social psychologist Leon Festinger introduced the Social Comparison Theory, which explains how we evaluate ourselves by comparing to others, whom we also see as better off. According to Festinger, this drive to compare is natural, and even necessary at times, but it becomes dangerous when it shifts from self-assessment to self-judgment.

❝

If you're always measuring yourself against people who appear more successful, attractive, or accomplished, it's easy to feel like you're falling short even if you're making meaningful progress.

These comparisons rarely tell the full story. They're snapshots, often based on assumptions and illusions. And yet, they carry enormous weight. Over time, they chip away at self-esteem and can paralyze our growth.

Unhappy People Compare More and It Hurts

This idea was expanded in a 1997 study by Sonja Lyubomirsky and Lee Ross. The researchers discovered a striking pattern: happy people were less affected by upward comparisons, while unhappy individuals felt significantly worse after comparing themselves to someone more successful. For the unhappy participants, seeing someone else do well reinforced their own feelings of inadequacy and failure.

This matters because it shows that comparison doesn't just reflect low confidence – it can actively contribute to it.

"

The more we compare, the worse we feel, and the worse we feel, the more we compare. It becomes a cycle that's hard to break unless we're intentional.

I love how Mel Robbins describes this in her book, *The Let Them Theory.* She once scrolled through social media and saw photos of her friends hanging out without her, laughing, dressed up, and having a great time. And there she was, alone on her couch with her dog, eating leftovers and feeling that familiar sting of comparison. Instantly, her mind spiraled: *Why didn't they invite me? Did I do something wrong?* She started overanalyzing, replaying conversations, and feeling left out. But then she caught herself and thought, *You know what? Let them.*

Let them go out. *Let them* have fun. *Let them* do whatever they want.

That small phrase stopped the emotional spiral in its tracks. She realized she could either spend the night resenting what others were doing or enjoy the peace of her own company, cozy, content, and free from the need to compare.

Comparison is sneaky like that. It tricks us into believing we're missing out, when in reality, we're just missing the joy of being completely present where we are.

Social Media: A Comparison Amplifier

In the digital age, the comparison trap is more accessible and more toxic than ever.

In a 2014 study published in *Psychology of Popular Media Culture*, researchers Ethan Vogel and colleagues found that greater Facebook use was associated with lower self-esteem, and this relationship was largely explained by social comparison. People who spent more time on social media were more likely to compare themselves to others and to come away feeling worse.

Think about it: we rarely post our bad days online. We curate our best angles, best moments, best milestones. When we compare ourselves to someone else's carefully edited highlight reel, we forget that we're measuring their front stage against our backstage.

The result? We feel behind. Unaccomplished. Not enough.

Progress Builds Confidence

So how do we rebuild our confidence?

Confidence doesn't come from comparison – it comes from progress. That's the insight behind The Progress Principle, a groundbreaking study by Teresa Amabile and Steven Kramer at Harvard Business School. They analyzed over 12,000 diary entries from professionals and found that the most powerful motivator at work wasn't money, recognition, or status. It was making progress in meaningful work, even small progress.

Every small win sends a message to your brain: *You're doing something right. Keep going.* And when you focus on your own growth, on becoming a little better than you were yesterday, you begin to trust yourself. That trust becomes confidence.

It's what the tortoise teaches us: you don't need to be fast, flashy, or perfect. You just need to keep moving.

The Power of Self-Compassion

Another antidote to comparison is self-compassion, a concept deeply researched by psychologist Kristin Neff. Unlike self-esteem, which often depends on feeling superior to others, self-compassion is about treating yourself with kindness in moments of difficulty or inadequacy.

Neff's research shows that people who practice self-compassion are less likely to engage in harmful comparisons, and more likely to persevere after setbacks. Why? Because instead of beating themselves up for not measuring up, they give themselves space to be human.

❝

Self-compassion doesn't make you complacent – it makes you resilient. It helps you recover faster, stay grounded, and keep running your race.

This is where the mini-shift comes in: **stop running everyone else's race, and run your own.**

Think of it like a marathon: every runner has a different body, pace, and strategy. If you spend the whole race glancing sideways, you waste energy and lose rhythm. The strongest runners wear blinders, not to ignore the competition, but to stay focused on their own stride.

That's the shift: redirecting your energy from measuring against others to building your own momentum.

For me, this lesson came after I left my corporate career.

For years, I had been an engineering leader. My days were packed with meetings, decisions, and hundreds of emails waiting for my attention. I was constantly in motion, leading teams, solving problems, driving results. My schedule was full, my title impressive, and my identity deeply tied to my work.

But when I stepped out to start my own business, everything changed. Suddenly, I went from being the one with answers to being a beginner again: learning marketing, building a website, figuring out social media, writing newsletters, networking, and creating from scratch.

It was humbling. And honestly, it was hard.

I kept looking around at others in my new field such as coaches, speakers, and authors who seemed so far ahead; and I inevitably compared. Their success stories made me question everything about myself. I told myself I wasn't smart enough, talented enough, or charismatic enough. More times than I can count, I whispered in my own head, *Maybe I'm just not cut out for this.*

But that's when the power of mentorship changed everything.

One day, during a conversation with my mentor Jack Canfield, he asked me a question that stopped me in my tracks.

He said, "Thanh, what brings you joy?"

I paused. The question seemed so simple, yet I hadn't asked myself that in a long time.

Jack continued, "Focus on the joy. Focus on serving others and doing what you do best. Don't compare your results with others; serve from your heart. The results will follow."

That conversation shifted something deep inside me. I realized that every time I compared myself to others, I was stepping out of my purpose and into someone else's. Confidence doesn't grow from comparison. It grows from alignment, from following your heart, and pursuing what brings you joy.

So, I turned my focus back to my lane, my work, my pace, and my purpose. I stopped trying to catch up to anyone and started showing up for the people I was meant to serve. And when I did that, I discovered something freeing:

❝

The only person I need to beat is the person I was yesterday.

SUGGESTED ACTION STEPS

I share many suggested action steps with you, but please don't feel you need to do them all at once. Just pick one step that resonates with you right now and take action on it. One small step forward is far more powerful than feeling overwhelmed and doing nothing.

You can't eliminate comparison completely because it's naturally wired into us. But you can reclaim your attention and energy with these research-backed practices:

- **Practice gratitude regularly**. In a study by *Emmons and McCullough (2003)*, people who kept gratitude journals reported higher levels of optimism and well-being and were less focused on what they lacked.

- **Be mindful of social media use**. In a 2015 study, *Fardouly et al.* found that even brief exposure to social media increased body dissatisfaction in young women. Curate your feed to follow accounts that uplift you, and take a break whenever you notice comparison or negativity creeping in.

- **Compare backward, not upward**. Instead of comparing to someone ahead of you, compare to your past self. Where were you a year ago? Celebrate how far you've come.

FINAL THOUGHTS

Like the tortoise, run your own race. Don't measure your life by someone else's pace. The only person you need to be better than is the person you were yesterday. Confidence doesn't come from comparison; it comes from clarity, consistency, and compassion.

So instead of measuring yourself against someone else's path, focus on your own. Define what success means to you. Celebrate how far you've come. And remember, the race isn't about who gets there first. It's about staying in motion, staying true to yourself, and not giving up.

What one small step do you commit to take to grow your confidence?

MINI-SHIFT #9:

Tiny Victories, Massive Momentum

"Acknowledge all of your small victories. They will eventually add up to something great."

– Kara Goucher

Many years ago, I felt stuck. Life felt heavy, and no matter how hard I worked or how much I achieved, I couldn't shake the feeling that nothing was going right. I was overwhelmed with negativity. My inner voice was filled with criticism. At work, I felt like everyone was against me. At home, I picked fights with my husband and found fault in everything he did. It felt like everything was falling apart.

Then I met Tom Jones.

He was the keynote speaker at a Toastmaster event I attended, and he shared a deeply moving story about overcoming addiction and completely turning his life around. His honesty, vulnerability, and transformation stirred something in me. After his talk, I stood at the back of a really long line of people waiting to talk to him, and I approached him and asked for guidance. I wasn't sure what I was looking for, but just that I needed a change. Because I was the last person at the end of the line, and it was already late, the conference was closing. Tom asked me if I would have dinner with him and his wife. I said yes. At dinner, Tom listened patiently for two hours as I poured my heart out. Then he asked me a question I'll never forget:

"Do you have anything in your life that you're grateful for?"

To my surprise, I went silent. I couldn't think of a single thing.

That's when he gave me a challenge: *"If you want me to mentor you, I want you to email me three things you're grateful for, first thing in the morning, every single day, for the next 30 days."*

I agreed, though I wasn't sure it would help.

At first, my gratitude list was painfully basic: *The air I breathe. The water I drink. The food I eat.*

But I kept emailing him. Day after day. After two weeks, something shifted.

I started noticing more things. I began writing: *My husband gave me a hug today. I had a peaceful moment during lunch. A coworker complimented my work.*

It felt like my eyes were opening to a world I hadn't seen in a while. The more good things I noticed, the more there was to notice. Gratitude wasn't just a practice; it was changing my brain.

By the end of 30 days, I was overflowing with appreciation.

I was no longer the same person. I had more energy, more clarity, and most importantly more joy.

This simple act of noticing and acknowledging small wins and being grateful for the blessings in my life, no matter how big or small, transformed my entire mindset. Gratitude began to shift the lens through which I saw the world. Instead of focusing on what was missing, I started to see what was already there. I realized that joy wasn't something I had to chase; it was something I could recognize, right where I was.

Little by little, the heaviness lifted. My thoughts softened. My relationships began to heal. The more I practiced gratitude, the more present I became and the more peace I found in ordinary moments. What had once felt like a life falling apart now felt like a life coming together, one thankful breath at a time.

Gratitude also laid the foundation for a powerful truth I've come to believe deeply: **confidence grows through small wins.**

We often think confidence comes from a big breakthrough, a promotion, a public award, or a flawless performance. But those moments are rare.

Lasting confidence isn't built in leaps but in tiny steps. Small wins create momentum. They signal to your brain: *I did that. I can do more.*

Those acknowledgments of gratitude built momentum for me. What I thought was just a gratitude exercise became something much bigger: a practice of confidence. Every small win I celebrated reminded me that I can do hard things – I am growing, I am enough.

"

This is the essence of a mini-shift: shifting from chasing rare lightning bolts to noticing everyday sparks. When you celebrate them, they add up, until your whole path is lit.

According to neuroscience research, when you experience a small success, your brain releases dopamine, often called the feel-good chemical. Dopamine not only creates pleasure; it also increases motivation and focus. It lights up your brain's reward center and says, *"Do that again."*

Studies from Harvard Medical School and Stanford University have shown that this release of dopamine reinforces goal-directed behavior, helping you stay engaged and resilient, even during challenges. Neuroscientist Dr. Andrew Huberman explains that celebrating small wins trains your brain to associate effort with reward, strengthening your motivation to keep going (Huberman, 2021). Similarly, Dr. Loretta Graziano Breuning, author of *Habits of a Happy Brain*, notes that when we intentionally celebrate small successes, we rewire our brains to create new pathways for joy and positivity (Breuning, 2015).

Gratitude and small victories are brain-training tools. Every moment of appreciation becomes a spark that rewires your brain toward optimism, confidence, and growth.

This chemical feedback loop reinforces the belief that your actions matter. And when you believe your actions matter, you take more of them, which fuels more progress, and more confidence.

"

This is the psychology of confidence: Celebrate → Feel good → Do more → Believe more → Become more.

Why We Overlook Small Wins

Many high achievers skip this step. They accomplish something and immediately move on to the next goal. They believe celebrating is indulgent or unnecessary. But when we fail to acknowledge progress, we rob ourselves of the internal motivation we need to keep going.

The Stoics would call this a trap of endless striving—a life spent chasing one thing after another without ever pausing to ask *why*. We confuse movement with meaning, quantity with quality, and busyness with purpose. In our pursuit to do more, we lose sight of what we've already become. Real growth isn't in constant motion; it's in awareness, gratitude, and presence.

I know this pattern well because I lived it.

For years, I would check one goal off the list only to replace it with three more. I told myself that pausing to celebrate was a waste of time. There was always another project, another milestone, another expectation waiting. When I earned my first patent, instead of feeling proud, I immediately thought about the next one. When I finished a major work presentation, I replayed every minor mistake instead of acknowledging that I had done something brave.

It's a mindset many high achievers share one rooted in striving rather than savoring. Our brains are wired to seek progress, but without moments of recognition, that constant striving becomes exhausting. It's like running a marathon without water breaks. Eventually, even the strongest runner slows down.

I remember one night after wrapping up a major project at work. Everyone was heading to dinner to celebrate, but I stayed behind, telling myself I had too much to do, and asking myself, "Is this all there is to life? Just one project after the next. One rung after another?"

The office was quiet except for the hum of the air conditioner and the glow of my computer screen. My inbox was full, but my heart felt empty. I had achieved what I once thought I wanted, which is a leadership title, a good salary, and recognition; yet something was missing. I was always chasing the next milestone but never pausing long enough to feel the joy of arriving.

That night, I realized I had become so focused on the summit that I forgot to enjoy the climb. I was measuring my worth by my output, not by the moments of growth, connection, or gratitude along the way. I was succeeding on paper but starving emotionally —because there is always another summit to ascend.

It took me years and the practice of gratitude to understand that fulfillment doesn't come from reaching the next goal; it comes from noticing the meaning in each step. When we celebrate small wins, we give ourselves permission to feel alive in the process, not just at the finish line.

Gratitude: The Sister Habit of Confidence

Gratitude and confidence are more connected than we realize. When you practice gratitude, you train your brain to look for what's good, what's working, and what you *can* do. When you focus on wins, even small ones, you replace helplessness with hope. Gratitude says, "I'm blessed." Confidence says, "I'm capable." Together, they say, "I have what it takes."

Over time, gratitude rewires your brain. According to research from UC Davis and UC Berkeley, people who keep a gratitude journal experience better sleep, lower stress, stronger immune systems, and more optimism about the future.

"

It's hard to feel like a failure when you're consistently noticing what you're doing right.

So how do you celebrate small wins without making it feel cheesy? Start simple. At the end of each day, write down one thing you did well, no matter how small.

When you complete a task you've been procrastinating, pause and say to yourself, *That was hard, but I did it.* Let others cheer for you – share your wins with a friend or coach.

Use visual cues like a win jar – write small victories on slips of paper and read them when you're feeling discouraged. Say thank you out loud when you notice a moment of peace, joy, or progress.

SUGGESTED ACTION STEPS

I share many suggested action steps with you, but please don't feel you need to do them all at once. Just pick one step that resonates with you right now and take action on it. One small step forward is far more powerful than feeling overwhelmed and doing nothing.

For tonight, reflect on these questions:
- *What is one small win you had today?*
- *How did it make you feel?*
- *Do you often give yourself credit for your progress?*
- *What could change if you celebrated your wins more intentionally?*

30-Day Gratitude Challenge

Just like Tom challenged me, I challenge you now:

For the next 30 days, write down three things you're grateful for every single day. Do it consistently because repetition builds new habits and new neural pathways. Over time, this simple practice trains your brain to recognize wins and joys in the little things: the blue sky above you, a blooming flower by the sidewalk, the green grass beneath your feet, someone holding the door open for you, or a warm smile during a tense meeting.

Gratitude rewires your focus from what's missing to what's meaningful, and that changes everything.

Even on the hard days when you feel like you have nothing to be grateful for, write something anyway. Can you still breathe? Do you have a roof over your head? A bed to sleep in? Food to fill your stomach? To many people, these simple things are extraordinary blessings. Gratitude isn't about having a perfect life; it's about recognizing the gifts that are already here, even in struggle.

You can write them in a journal, a note on your phone, or even send them to someone you trust. Don't worry if they feel small or repetitive. This practice isn't about variety but about building a new habit.

You may be surprised by how your mind begins to shift.

You'll look for the good; and in doing so, realizing your own strength, growth, and resilience.

If you'd like a dedicated space to record your reflections, I've created several gratitude journals designed to help you build this habit. They include prompts, space for daily notes, and inspiring reminders to keep you going. You can buy the hard copies here https://www.amazon.com/author/thanhnguyen, or download a free pdf at https://www.theencourageteam.com/FreeResources

FINAL THOUGHTS

Confidence doesn't come from standing at the top of the mountain. It comes from taking the next step and noticing that you did. So celebrate. Every step. Every effort. Every breath of courage. You don't need to wait for the big win to believe in yourself – you just need to start seeing the small ones already happening.

What one small step do you commit to take to grow your confidence?

MINI-SHIFT #10:

Breathe. Align. Rise

"Confidence isn't just in your mind.
It's in your muscles, your breath,
your vision, and your voice."

– Kobe Bryant

Have you ever been in a meeting when your boss asked if anyone had ideas to share, and you knew deep down that you had a great one, but you just couldn't bring yourself to speak up?

Your palms started to sweat. Your heart raced. The thought of raising your hand and standing in front of the room felt like too much. So you stayed quiet. Even though you had something valuable to say.

Or maybe you're like my talented friend, a brilliant nurse, who was invited to do Facebook Live to talk about a topic she's an expert in. She knows the content backward and forward, but she was so terrified she lost sleep for days leading to it.

If you've ever felt this fear around speaking in public, you're not alone. Studies have shown that the fear of public speaking ranks as the #1 phobia for adults, even higher than the fear of death! Three out of four adults experience anxiety when speaking publicly. So if you're afraid of public speaking, welcome to the club. You're just like us, normal people.

As Nelson Mandela once said, *"Courage is not the absence of fear, but the triumph over it."* That quote has stayed with me for years, because I believe it's absolutely true. You can fear public speaking and *still* give a meaningful talk that adds real value to your audience.

My Turning Point

Early in my career, I mistakenly believed that as an engineer, my job was only about data and reports. I thought I could stay behind the scenes, crunch numbers, and let my work speak for itself. I underestimated the power of communicating well, speaking up in public and networking with others.

That mistake cost me. I worked for a manager who regularly belittled me, questioned my intelligence, and made me feel small. And because I struggled with public speaking, I stayed quiet, even when I had good ideas to contribute. That silence slowly eroded my self-esteem.

But I refused to stay stuck. As I shared in earlier chapters, I joined Toastmasters and started practicing. I pushed myself to speak, even when my hands were shaking and my voice trembling. With time, things began to shift. I grew more comfortable sharing ideas. I started forming professional relationships. My confidence grew, and that manager's influence over me began to shrink. Eventually, I moved into a different role, away from his toxicity.

Public speaking didn't just help me find my voice. It helped me *change my path*.

Over the years I've refined a simple ritual that steadies me before any talk, class, or meeting: **practice, focus on the audience, and align my breath, body, and mind.**

This last part, the alignment, is how confidence moves from something you think about to something you embody.

Let's explore this.

When we experience anxiety about public speaking, it's often because we're focused on ourselves:

- *Will I forget my words?*
- *Will they think I'm boring?*

- *What if I sound stupid?*
- *What if I fail?*

All these fears are tied to our self-image, how we *think* we'll appear in the eyes of others. That pressure can feel crushing. Our bodies respond as if we're in danger: rapid heartbeat, sweaty palms, shaking hands, and even dizziness.

So the question is: How can we calm our nerves and show up as our most confident selves?

By engaging the full power of our body, mind, and voice. The trio that works best for me is simple: **Breathe. Posture. Visualize.** Then seal it with **Affirmation**.

Breathe First

When we're nervous, anxious, or doubting ourselves, our breath is often the first thing to change, shallow, rapid, and tight. But taking a single deep breath can shift everything.

Deep Breath Creates Space to Regulate Emotions

A deep breath gives us a pause button. It creates a moment between stimulus and response and gives us a space to calm ourselves instead of reacting impulsively. Confidence isn't about never feeling fear; it's about responding with composure in the face of fear. A deep breath grounds us in the present moment and interrupts the spiraling thoughts that often trigger insecurity.

Deep Breath Activates the Body's Relaxation Response

Breathing deeply activates the parasympathetic nervous system, which slows the heart rate and relaxes the body. This physical response signals to the brain: *You are safe*. When we feel safe, we think more clearly, speak more calmly, and show up more confidently.

Deep Breath Anchors Us in the Present

So much of self-doubt comes from dwelling on past mistakes or worrying about the future.

"

A deep breath anchors us right here, right now. And confidence lives in the present, not in the what-ifs, but in the "I am."

Power Postures

Harvard researcher Amy Cuddy popularized the idea that **how you hold your body changes how you feel**. In her well-known TED Talk, she shares how power posing, such as taking up space, standing tall, and expanding your posture, can reduce cortisol (the stress hormone) and increase testosterone (associated with confidence and assertiveness).

When you assume a powerful stance, even if you don't feel confident at first, your brain starts to follow suit. You begin to feel more assured, more capable, more grounded.

So before you speak, **stand tall**. Roll your shoulders back. Plant your feet firmly. Raise your arms in a victorious "V" shape or stand like Wonder Woman with your hands on your hips. Hold that posture for two minutes. Breathe deeply. Own your space.

Visualization

Olympic athletes use visualization to mentally rehearse their routines. Why? Because the brain can't easily distinguish between something vividly imagined and something actually experienced.

When you visualize yourself succeeding, walking confidently into the room, making eye contact, hearing the audience respond warmly, you're preparing your brain to *believe* that outcome is possible. You're giving it a script to follow.

Close your eyes and picture yourself doing well. Imagine feeling proud at the end of your talk. Let that version of you lead the way.

Affirmation

We all have an inner voice, and for some of us, that voice is loud and critical. But it doesn't have to stay that way.

Affirmations are intentional phrases you say to yourself to replace fear with strength. They help you speak *to* your brain rather than *from* your fear.

Right before I speak, I repeat affirmations like:

- *I am prepared and calm.*
- *I have something valuable to share.*
- *This isn't about me. It's about serving others.*
- *My voice matters.*

And then I say a short prayer:

Dear God, please allow me to add value to my audience. They've sacrificed their time to listen to me. Please help me use my voice to the best of my ability to add value to them.

These words help center me, not on performance, but on purpose.

Aligning Breath, Body, and Mind

Confidence isn't only in the mind – it's carried in the body.

I discovered that when I began paying attention to breath and posture. A deep inhale steadied my nerves, and standing tall made me feel taller inside. Lowering my shoulders and grounding my feet gave me strength before I said a word.

Think of it like tuning a musical instrument. When one string is off, the whole sound feels shaky. But when breath, body, and mind are in tune, you project harmony and confidence.

This practice doesn't erase nerves. I still get butterflies before I speak. But now, instead of fighting them, I align them. Breath becomes rhythm. Posture becomes presence. Mind becomes focus. Together, they transform shaky energy into steady power.

That's what makes this a mini-shift: not forcing yourself to *feel* confident but physically aligning yourself so your body leads your mind there.

SUGGESTED ACTION STEPS

I share many suggested action steps with you, but please don't feel you need to do them all at once. Just pick one step that resonates with you right now and take action on it. One small step forward is far more powerful than feeling overwhelmed and doing nothing.

Here's a simple 3-minute routine you can try before your next big moment:

Take a Few Deep Breaths

You may recite this poem from the Zen master, Thich Nhat Hanh:

Breathing in, I calm my body.
Breathing out, I smile.
Dwelling in the present moment,
I know this is a wonderful moment.

Strike a Power Pose

Stand tall. Feet shoulder-width apart. Hands on hips or raised in a "V".

Hold for two minutes. Breathe deeply.

Visualize Your Success

Close your eyes and picture the event going well. See yourself smiling, connecting, and finishing with pride.

Affirm Your Strength

Repeat your personal affirmation. Say a prayer or a mantra that centers you in service, not fear.

Reflection Questions

When was the last time you let fear stop you from speaking up?

How does your body feel when you're nervous? Can you recognize the signs early?

What image would help you feel more confident before your next challenge?

Write an affirmation that speaks directly to your self-doubt. What do you need to hear?

FINAL THOUGHTS

I once heard a great speaker, Ryan Leak, share that he still feels nervous before speaking. That really resonated with me. I had been in Toastmasters for years and had delivered many speeches in front of large audiences, and I still get butterflies every time I step on stage. But I've learned something important: nerves aren't a sign of weakness; they're a sign that you care.

Feeling nervous means you want to do well. It means your message matters. So instead of fighting the butterflies, let them remind you that you're alive, growing, and doing something meaningful.

What matters is how you *prepare*.

Use your body to shift your energy. Use your imagination to pave the way. Use your voice to remind yourself who you are and what you bring. Align your body, mind, and voice, and watch your confidence rise.

You don't have to wait until you feel confident. You can *train* yourself to feel confident. And it starts right here, right now, with one deep breath and the choice to show up anyway.

What one small step do you commit taking to grow your confidence?

MINI-SHIFT #11:

Keep Becoming

"I have not failed. I've just found 10,000 ways that won't work."

- Thomas Edison

The applause was still echoing in my ears.

I had just stepped off the stage, heart racing with excitement. After months of preparation, my talk had gone exactly as I'd hoped. People lined up to thank me, telling me how my words resonated with them and gave them hope. I felt proud and maybe even a little relieved.

When I got to my car, I called my coach, Roddy Galbraith, founder of *Speaker Pro* and a faculty mentor with the *Maxwell Leadership Team*. "It went great!" I said, still smiling.

"Congratulations," he replied warmly. Then came the question I almost expected to hear because he had asked it after every time I spoke on stage.

"Did you get the recording?"

I hesitated. "Yes…"

"Good," he said. "Let's watch it together and see how we can make it even better."

Although I already kind of expected it, I still froze.

"Oh no, Roddy. I can't watch it. I'm scared. I'll see every awkward moment, every mistake."

Inside, I thought, *Can't we just leave it at, I did a good job, the audience said so, and move on?*

He laughed softly, but his tone carried wisdom.

"Yes, you can, Thanh. You're a professional. And as a professional, you must watch your recording to grow. Even a second of improvement matters. Your audience deserves your best. Think of athletes," he continued. "They watch their games and their performances over and over again, not because they enjoy seeing themselves on screen, but because excellence requires awareness."

99

In that moment, I realized something powerful: confidence isn't about perfection. It's about progress. True confidence grows when we stop fearing our flaws and start learning from them.

A growth mindset is exactly that, a way of seeing ourselves not as finished products, but as works in progress. It's the belief that every challenge, mistake, or piece of feedback isn't proof of inadequacy, but an opportunity to improve.

That day, I stopped chasing perfection and started chasing growth.

When I began learning public speaking, I thought people were born just naturally good at it. That some had the gift of communication, and others, like me at the time, were meant to stay quiet in the back row. I thought to myself, *I'm the engineer type who is good at math, and people like me aren't good at words.*

It's the same belief I had when I was learning piano as a child or when I struggled to write in English after moving to the United States. I remember sitting at my desk in school, watching classmates raise their hands with ease while I panicked silently, trying to figure out if I even understood the question. I would beat myself up every time I got something wrong, thinking, *I might not ever get good at speaking English. Language is not my forte.*

I thought if I wasn't naturally good at something, it meant I was never going to be. But I was wrong: what I didn't realize at the time was that this belief that talent is fixed, that struggle is a sign to quit, that failure is fatal, is part of what Dr. Carol Dweck, a Stanford psychologist, calls a **fixed mindset**.

People with a fixed mindset believe their abilities are set in stone. That intelligence, creativity, confidence, and even leadership are all traits you either have or you don't. They avoid challenges because challenges might expose their limitations, and they give up easily because setbacks feel like proof they're not enough. They see effort as pointless – after all, if you're talented, why would you need to try so hard?

But people with a growth mindset believe that abilities can be developed. That we can learn, grow, improve, and evolve through dedication and effort. They embrace challenges, persist through failure, and see mistakes not as dead ends but as invitations to level up.

Shifting from a fixed mindset to a growth mindset was one of the most powerful acts of confidence I've ever taken. It completely transformed how I approached public speaking and life.

Let's look closely at the difference.

A fixed mindset says:

- *I'm not good at math.*
- *I'm not a leader.*
- *I'm not confident.*
- *I can't do this.*

A growth mindset says:

- *I'm not good at math* yet.

- *I'm learning how to lead.*
- *I'm building my confidence.*
- *I don't know how to do this* yet, *but I'm willing to try.*

A growth mindset shifts the story you tell yourself from final to flexible, from stuck to still growing. It reminds you that you're a work in progress, not a finished product.

Confidence doesn't come from always succeeding. It comes from knowing that you'll keep growing even when you fall short. And it comes from trusting that your best today doesn't define your ceiling, and that it only defines your starting line.

When Criticism Became My Wake-Up Call

In 2008, I became a mom for the first time. Like most new mothers, I was exhausted, overwhelmed, and still adjusting to my new life. I hadn't budgeted enough time for maternity leave, so just weeks after giving birth, I had to return to work. Between hormonal changes, sleepless nights, feeding my colicky baby, and the heartbreak of leaving her at daycare, I wasn't ready. Not even close.

Then, only weeks into my return, my boss called me into that meeting, telling me I ranked at the bottom of the team. For someone who had always been a high achiever, this experience crushed me.

I was already carrying mom guilt. My daughter wasn't adjusting well to daycare and cried for hours after I left. I felt torn between wanting to be home and wanting to keep my career. That performance review nearly broke me. I considered quitting.

Why did it hurt so much? Because negative feedback hits us on two levels:

Right Brain (emotions, belonging): It makes us feel unloved, rejected, disconnected. We crave acceptance, so criticism feels like a threat to our relationships.

Left Brain (logic, ability): It makes us feel incompetent or unworthy, striking at our need to feel capable and valuable.

That's why criticism feels like a double punch: it shakes both our sense of belonging and our sense of worth.

But here's the turning point: even though every part of me wanted to resist his criticism, and even after discovering that he had said similar things to other women engineers, revealing his bias, I still forced myself to dig deeper: Was there any truth in what he said?

The answer was yes. I realized that while I hadn't been coasting, I also wasn't giving it my best. Somewhere along the way, I had assumed that once I graduated and landed a job, the hardest work was behind me. Without even realizing it, I had slipped into a fixed mindset. As John Maxwell says, "Everything worthwhile is uphill." Growth requires continuous effort.

That performance review became my wake-up call. Within four years, I earned not just one, but two master's degrees — a master's in engineering and later an Executive MBA. On graduation day, my kids decorated my cap with Olaf from Frozen to give me extra height on stage. Watching them jumping up and down, screaming "Mom. Go Mom," from the audience seats as I walked across the stage remains one of my proudest moments: a symbol of resilience, growth, and refusing to let criticism define me.

My Own Growth Mindset Moment

One of the biggest mindset shifts I had was when I stopped measuring my worth based on performance and started measuring it based on growth.

When I began speaking at conferences, I remember feeling completely out of place. I would sit backstage watching seasoned speakers with polished delivery, perfect timing, captivating stories, and booming applause. I would wonder, *What am I doing here? I don't sound like them. I don't have their stage presence.*

The imposter syndrome crept in quickly. I compared myself to everyone else and felt small in comparison. But then I remembered something important. I remembered the first speech I gave at Toastmasters, how I stood behind the lectern, trembling, reading from a piece of paper without making eye contact. My voice shook. My hands did too. I couldn't wait to finish.

What happened between that moment and the one I was in now wasn't magic — it was growth.

Years of Toastmasters meetings. Countless speeches. Endless rounds of feedback about every um, ah, like, or so. I worked with speaking coaches, took notes, rewrote, rehearsed, and showed up again and again. Each time, I pushed myself a little further out of my comfort zone, raising my hand to speak, volunteering for speaking contests, and saying yes to opportunities that terrified me.

I learned to speak with heart.

To focus less on myself and more on the audience.

To find meaning in making a difference through my words.

And now? Here I was, on a stage, without a script, sharing stories from my life, looking into people's eyes and making them laugh, pause, and reflect.

Was I perfect? No. Was I growing? Absolutely. And that became my new measuring stick.

Instead of comparing myself to others, I began comparing myself to who I was yesterday. Instead of asking, *Am I as good as them?* I started asking, *Am I better than I was last time?*

That's when everything changed.

The only person you need to compete with is the person you used to be.

Three Steps to Turn Feedback into Growth Fuel

Here's the framework I use – and now teach – to turn criticism into confidence:

Step 1: Pause and Vent Safely

- Don't react immediately.
- Vent to a trusted person (your spouse, coach, or friend who will listen without judgment).
- Tell them upfront: *I just need to vent. I'm not asking for advice. I just need your loving, supportive listening ears.*
- Avoid venting to someone who works in the same place as you. When we receive negative feedback, it's natural to react emotionally, but in that state, we may

miscommunicate or say things we don't truly mean. This can easily slip into gossip and, unintentionally, end up hurting someone else.

Step 2: Sort the Feedback into 3 Buckets

- Totally Unfair → Drop it. Don't carry what doesn't belong to you.
- Truth → Accept it. Ask, *What's one small step I can take to grow from this?*
- Grey Area (Perception) → Decide. You can either:
  1. Shift perception: change how you show up to avoid misunderstanding, or
  2. Clarify directly: ask for a follow-up conversation.

Step 3: Reframe It as Growth Fuel

Feedback is information, not a verdict. When you reflect instead of react, you stay in control. And even unfair criticism can build your confidence – if you choose to use it.

Feedback is just a moment. Growth is the journey.
Don't let a moment in time ruin your journey.

Even Giants Stumbled

Some of the most iconic figures in history didn't succeed because they were naturally confident, and they became confident because they learned how to fail, grow, and keep going.

- **Abraham Lincoln** lost many elections, failed in business, and suffered personal tragedies before becoming one of the most respected presidents in U.S. history.
- **Walt Disney** was fired by a newspaper editor who said he "lacked imagination and had no good ideas." His early ventures failed. Yet he didn't give up and created one of the most imaginative worlds ever known.
- **Michael Jordan** was cut from his high school basketball team. Jordan used the rejection as motivation. He later became one of the greatest basketball players in history, often crediting failure as a key to his success.
- **Howard Schultz**, the founder of Starbucks, was turned down by 242 banks when trying to get funding for his coffee shop concept. He persisted, and Starbucks is now a global brand.

What made these individuals extraordinary wasn't the absence of failure but their refusal to let failure define them. They embodied a growth mindset, believing that effort, persistence, and learning from mistakes would lead to success.

That same mindset is available to you. Confidence doesn't come from knowing you'll always get it right, but from knowing you'll keep going and improving.

Growth is happening, even when you don't see it in the moment.

It's like tending a garden. Seeds don't sprout overnight. They need water, sunlight, and care. Some wilt before they bloom. But every effort teaches you how to cultivate better. The same is true for confidence: every attempt, even the ones that fall flat, grows something in you.

That's the mini-shift here: moving from asking, *Am I good at this?* to asking, *What can I do to get good?* One question closes doors; the other opens them wide.

SUGGESTED ACTION STEPS

I share many suggested action steps with you, but please don't feel you need to do them all at once. Just pick one step that resonates with you right now and take action on it. One small step forward is far more powerful than feeling overwhelmed and doing nothing.

Growth Mindset in Action

So how do you adopt a growth mindset and make it a daily part of your life? Start here:

1. Reframe failure as feedback

Every mistake holds a message. When something doesn't go as planned, don't label it a failure but treat it as feedback. Ask yourself:

- *What did I learn?*
- *What can I do differently next time?*
- *How can I grow from this?*

I like to call it failing forward. Because even when you fall, you're still moving.

2. Add "yet" to your language

This simple shift rewires how you think.

Instead of: *I don't know how to do this,* say: *I don't know how to do this* yet.

When you start adding the word yet, *I'm not good at this... yet,* you train your brain to expect growth. And that expectation builds resilience, which builds confidence.

3. Celebrate effort, not just outcome

We're conditioned to celebrate results such as grades, trophies, and promotions. But real confidence is built in the unseen moments: the late-night studying, the hundredth rehearsal, the times you wanted to quit but didn't.

Clap for yourself when you try. Celebrate every step forward. Progress deserves just as much applause as perfection.

4. Practice self-compassion

Let's be honest. Growth is messy. You'll have days when you feel stuck, when you stumble, when you make mistakes. Talk to yourself the way you'd talk to a friend.

You wouldn't say to a friend, "You're such a failure." You'd say, "This is hard, but I'm proud of you for trying."

Say that to yourself, too.

5. Track your progress

Keep a journal, a note on your phone, or even a voice memo log. Record things you tried that scared you. Reflect on what you learned. Make a habit of noticing how far you've come.

Take some time today to sit with these questions and write down your responses:

What is something you once believed you weren't good at but learned through practice?

Where do you still carry a fixed mindset about yourself?

What's one area of your life where you can start adding the word "yet"?

What mistake in your life turned out to be a powerful lesson?

FINAL THOUGHTS

You are not a finished product; you are a beautiful work in progress. You're growing through every stumble, every awkward attempt, every moment you feel like you're not quite there yet. You're evolving; you're becoming someone stronger, wiser, and more confident than you were yesterday. When you adopt a growth mindset, failure stops feeling like rejection and starts feeling like refinement.

You don't have to be perfect; you just have to be willing. You don't have to have all the answers; you just have to keep asking questions. You don't have to win every time, you just have to keep showing up.

Let the goal be growth, not perfection. Let your confidence be rooted not in being the best but in becoming your best. One challenge at a time. One lesson at a time. One courageous step at a time.

What one small step do you commit to take to grow your confidence?

MINI-SHIFT #12:

You Don't Have to Grow Alone

"Surround yourself with people who lift you higher."

– Oprah Winfrey

Have you ever noticed how some people make you feel like you can do anything, while others make you second-guess everything?

There are people whose presence lifts you, whose words energize you, and whose belief in you becomes a mirror in which you see your own strength. And then there are those whose doubts, sarcasm, and small-mindedness chip away at your confidence, bit by bit.

66

*That's why one of the most important choices you can make for your growth is this: **choose the people around you intentionally.***

Jim Rohn famously said, *"You are the average of the five people you spend the most time with."* I didn't fully understand the depth of that statement until I started reflecting on my own life, on the times when I doubted myself, and on the people who believed in me when I couldn't believe in myself. Their encouragement, faith, and example reminded me that confidence is often borrowed before it's built.

When I was a junior-level engineer, I had the honor of being mentored by one of the most respected leaders in our company, our highest-ranking engineer, Dr. Altuve. He was brilliant, with decades of experience and a reputation that made even the most senior professionals notice when he entered a room.

And yet, when he met with me, he didn't carry himself with superiority or ego. He greeted me warmly every single time and would say things like, *"It's always great to talk with such an incredibly smart engineer like you."*

I struggled with confidence, often minimizing my own accomplishments, downplaying my ideas, or criticizing myself out loud. I'd say things like, *"I probably should've caught that mistake,* or *I'm still figuring it out; I'm not that good."*

Every time I did, he would gently correct me. He'd stop and say, *"Don't talk like that. You're smart. You're capable. You're learning, yes, but don't forget you're already bringing a lot of value."*

That encouragement made a deep impression on me. He didn't just mentor my skills; he mentored my **self-perception**. He saw something in me before I saw it in myself, and he helped me start seeing it too.

Supportive people do that. They don't let you stay small; they remind you of your worth when you forget. And they correct your self-doubt with truth and kindness.

I'm fortunate to have a friend and business partner who embodies this principle, Mark Hemingway.

Mark is one of those rare people who *choose* to see the good in everyone. Every time I talk to him, he gives at least 30 seconds of genuine praise. Not flattery but encouragement rooted in truth. He notices your effort. He highlights your strengths, and in doing so, he lifts your belief in yourself.

When you're around Mark, you feel seen, valued, and inspired. That's the person you want on your journey. Supportive people don't just cheer you on; they *see* your potential and call it out. They speak belief into your life until you can borrow their belief long enough to find your own.

To build confidence, don't go it alone. Find encouragers. Be an encourager. Because when someone believes in you, it helps you believe in yourself, and that's where confidence begins.

The Patent Story: Two Voices, One Choice

Many years ago, I was listed on my first patent. That was a proud moment that symbolized years of dedication, collaboration, and effort. But the moment didn't go quite as expected.

Another engineer, someone I had worked alongside, made a comment that stung more than I'd like to admit. With a smirk, he said, *"You probably just smiled your way through it. That's why your name's on the patent."*

I was stunned. In one sentence, he dismissed my intelligence, my contribution, and my effort. He reduced my achievement to charm. It was a subtle jab wrapped in a joke, but it landed like a punch.

My confidence wavered. For a moment, I questioned myself. *Was I really good enough to be listed? Had I truly contributed enough?*

But then my co-inventor stepped in. He pulled me aside later and said, *"As far as I'm concerned, you are a full contributor to this patent. I saw the work you did. You absolutely earned this."*

And just like that, I was reminded: One voice can plant doubt, but another can restore belief.

"

That moment taught me something I'll never forget: **Who you listen to matters.** *Not everyone deserves access to your heart, your dreams, or your story.*

Confidence is not built in isolation. The words, energy, and presence of the people around us shape it. If your environment is filled with gossip, criticism, cynicism, and small thinking, even the strongest self-belief can begin to crack.

But if you surround yourself with people who uplift, encourage, and challenge you with love, you'll begin to rise. You'll stretch into your potential. You'll take risks, speak up, and show up differently because we tend to live up or down to the expectations of the people around us. That's why your circle matters.

Confidence may begin within you, but it never grows in isolation. Who you walk beside shapes how boldly you walk.

I've had seasons in my life when I was surrounded by people who doubted, criticized, or dismissed me. No matter how much I tried to hold on to confidence, it slipped away in that environment. And I've had other seasons when I was surrounded by encouragers, mentors, colleagues, and friends who saw more in me than I saw in myself. Their belief became my bridge until I could believe in myself.

> 66
>
> *Think of it like a campfire: alone, a single flame*
> *flickers and fades, but gathered together, flames feed*
> *each other, creating warmth and light that none*
> *could produce alone. The same is true of confidence*
> *– with the right people around you, your fire grows*
> *brighter.*

For My Fellow Introverts

If you're an introvert, this message might feel especially personal. I understand because I've always been one too.

Building your circle doesn't mean attending large networking events, being the center of attention, or showing up on a big stage surrounded by people. It can be done one meaningful connection at a time.

Introverts actually have a beautiful advantage in relationship building: we usually thrive in one-on-one settings. Our conversations are often deeper, more thoughtful, and more genuine. We listen intently. We connect through understanding, not performance.

Some of the strongest relationships I've built began not at conferences or in big crowds, but over coffee, through quiet conversations, or even heartfelt messages exchanged online.

So if you're an introvert, don't feel pressured to be loud to be seen. You can build your circle quietly, intentionally, and authentically. Because confidence doesn't require a crowd, it grows through connection.

Sometimes, one genuine relationship can do more for your confidence than a hundred casual acquaintances ever could.

That's why this mini-shift matters: it's about shifting from trying to carry your confidence alone to choosing the circle that fuels you.

And if you don't yet have that kind of circle, don't lose heart. Start by becoming it: be the encourager, the truth-teller, the believer for someone else. That energy not only strengthens them, but it also attracts the kind of community you've been searching for.

SUGGESTED ACTION STEPS

I share many suggested action steps with you, but please don't feel you need to do them all at once. Just pick one step that resonates with you right now and take action on it. One small step forward is far more powerful than feeling overwhelmed and doing nothing.

How to Build a Confidence-Boosting Circle

To grow your confidence, start by curating your environment, especially your relationships. Here's how:

1. Seek Out Builders, Not Breakers
Spend time with people who:
- Speak hope and encouragement
- Celebrate your growth and effort
- Tell you the truth with kindness
- Reflect your strengths, not your flaws

You'll know you've found them when you leave a conversation feeling seen, empowered, and energized.

2. Limit Time with Drainers

You don't need to cut people off, but you can protect your peace. Be mindful of:

- Constant complainers
- People who mock ambition
- Those who talk behind others' backs
- Anyone who consistently leaves you doubting yourself

Energy is contagious. Choose yours wisely.

3. Find Growth-Minded Communities

If your current circle isn't supportive, go find one that is. Consider joining one or more of these groups:

- Toastmasters
- Rotary International, Lions Club, or Kiwanis — international organizations that focus on service, leadership, and community impact
- Mastermind or coaching circles
- Faith communities or values-based meetups
- Volunteer teams or wellness groups

Being around people who are growing will inspire your own growth.

4. Ask for Encouragement (and Give It Too)

Sometimes all it takes is letting someone know you need support. Say, *"I'm struggling with this; can I talk it through with you?"*

And remember to be that supportive person for others. The more you give, the more you attract.

5. Be the Person You're Looking For

Confidence is magnetic. So is kindness. When you become the kind of person who uplifts others, you naturally begin to attract the same energy.

Reflection Exercise

Take a moment to reflect:

- *Who are the five people I spend the most time with? How do they make me feel?*
- *Who has poured belief into me when I needed it most?*
- *Are there relationships I need to set healthy boundaries around?*
- *What group or person could I reach out to that reflects the kind of growth I'm pursuing?*
- *How can I be more like my mentor, or my co-inventor, for someone else?*

FINAL THOUGHTS

You don't have to build confidence alone. Yes, much of the journey comes from within, from mindset shifts, daily habits, and learning to believe in yourself. But who walks beside you on that journey makes all the difference. Choose people who reflect your light, not your shadows. People who challenge you to grow, not to shrink. People who speak your name with respect, not ridicule.

And if you haven't found those people yet, don't worry. Start becoming one of them instead. Start showing up as the encourager, the believer, the truth-teller, and the builder because that kind of energy doesn't just change you. It attracts the community you've been searching for.

Your circle matters. Your voice matters. And you deserve to be surrounded by people who see your worth, even when you forget. Confidence grows in the presence of love, truth, and belief.

So choose to be, and be with, people who help you rise. Surround yourself with people who remind you of your strength, not your shortcomings.

What one small step do you commit to taking to grow your confidence?

CONCLUSION:

Life Happens in a Blink

You know how life can change in an instant, right?

One moment everything feels normal, predictable, in rhythm, and then the next...everything's different.

That's how fragile life really is. Sometimes the reminders are gentle. Other times, they crash into you.

A few years ago, my husband and I took our children – Valerie, 8, and William, 6 – on a trip to Vietnam. We wanted to show them where we grew up.

From the moment we arrived, they were captivated: the motorbikes weaving through narrow streets, the street vendors calling out, the scent of fresh fruit and grilled food. It was new and exhilarating for them. Every day was a sensory adventure.

After a week of exploring, we headed to one of Vietnam's beautiful beaches. The days were warm and slow, filled with sandcastles, laughter, and family joy. It was the kind of experience you tuck into your memory for safekeeping.

Then, in one second, everything changed.

We were walking down the street one evening, hand in hand. I was holding William's hand when, without warning, I disappeared.

The ground beneath me gave way. Everything went dark.

I had fallen into a manhole.

I hit a pipe on the way down, and my body was in shock. All I could hear was William's screams and my husband shouting for help. In that terrifying moment, one question pulsed in my mind:

Have I done enough? Have I prepared my children if I'm not here tomorrow?

After what felt like forever, someone lowered a rope, and I was pulled up. Bruised, bleeding, and shaken, but alive. The look on William's face when I emerged from that hole is burned into my memory: he was pale, silent, and frozen in fear.

We later learned the manhole had been under construction. It had been covered with a piece of glass and hidden under dirt. William had walked across it moments before, but he was so small and light that nothing happened. But when I stepped on it, the glass shattered.

That moment became one of those "before and after" events in my life.

The Turning Point

Later that night, back at the hotel, I couldn't sleep. I sat on the balcony under a blanket of stars, overwhelmed not by pain, but by perspective. I kept thinking, *What have I been putting off? Why do we live like we have forever? What would I regret if I didn't return from something as simple as a walk?*

That experience reminded me how easily we postpone the things that matter: our dreams, our health, our relationships, our self-expression. We tell ourselves we'll get to it later. When things slow down. When we feel more ready. When life gives us a better moment.

But life doesn't always give us more moments. And often, it's not about the right time, but the right choice.

The Illusion of Someday

I've seen too many people wait.

They wait to use their voice until they feel more confident. They wait to take the trip, have the conversation, apply for the job, start the project because life is just too busy.

We get caught in the pull of the urgent. We respond to everyone else's needs, put out fires, handle the crisis, check our notifications, and then wonder where the time went.

That night, as I reflected, I remembered Stephen Covey's four quadrants of time:

- *Quadrant 1: Urgent and Important* – real emergencies, deadlines, and problems.
- *Quadrant 2: Not Urgent but Important* – health, purpose, family, goals, personal growth.
- *Quadrant 3: Urgent but Not Important* – interruptions, some meetings, social expectations.
- *Quadrant 4: Not Urgent and Not Important* – mindless scrolling, distractions, time-wasters.

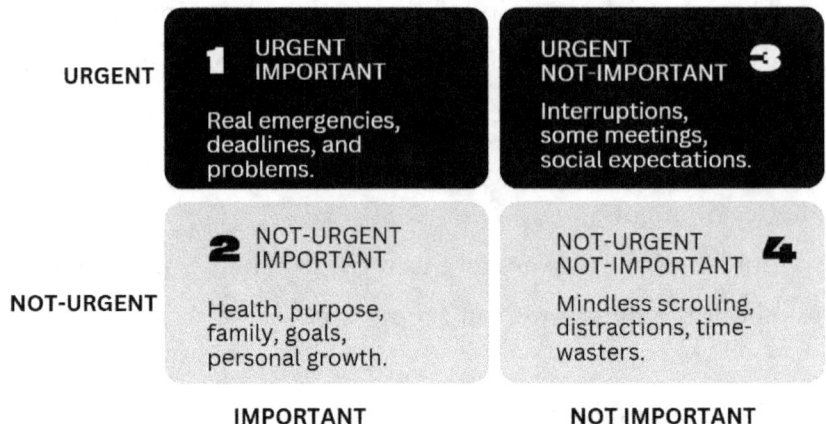

Most people live in Quadrants 1, 3, and 4. They are always reacting, always responding, always busy, or just drifting through life, unknowingly wasting their most precious commodity that is time. We can earn many things in life, but not time. Once time is gone, it's gone.

But the life that actually matters happens in Quadrant 2.

That's where we care for our health. That's where we connect deeply with the people we love. That's where we plant seeds for our legacy, our creativity, our meaning. That's where confidence is born, not from crisis, but from intention.

The Final Mini-Shift: Urgency

This book has walked you through 12 mini-shifts, small, intentional changes that build confidence one degree at a time. And here, at the close, I want to leave you with one more: the mini-shift of urgency.

"

Don't wait. Don't hide. Don't assume you have endless tomorrows. A shift doesn't have to be grand; it just has to be now. Just as a plane changes its entire destination by altering course by a single degree, you can change the trajectory of your life by taking one courageous step today.

Light Was Never Meant to Be Hidden

There's a simple, universal truth: every person carries a light inside them. Call it your spark, your gift, your wisdom, your story, your voice, whatever language fits your worldview. But it's there.

And too often, we hide it. We hesitate to speak because we don't want to be wrong. We hold back from creating because we think we're not good enough. We dim our personalities, ideas, and dreams to fit in, not stand out.

But the light in you? It was never meant to be buried. The world needs people who live lit up from within. Who are bold enough to shine, especially in dark times. Who inspire others by their presence, their words, and their choices.

You may never know how your courage will impact someone else. But it does.

Every time you show up authentically...

Every time you choose growth over fear...

Every time you step out when it would be easier to stay quiet...

You send out light. And light spreads.

Someone Is Waiting for Your Bravery

There's someone out there who needs your story. Someone who needs your smile. Someone who needs your perspective, your encouragement, your leadership. When you shine, you don't just light your own path; you light the way for others.

You might not think you're qualified. You might not feel ready. But here's the secret: **you don't have to be perfect to be powerful. You just have to be willing.**

Confidence Is a Choice. One You Can Make Today.

You've made it through 12 mini-shifts. You've reflected, wrestled, and practiced. You've read stories – mine and maybe some of your own. Each shift invited you to see yourself differently, to let go of self-doubt, and to take small, courageous steps toward confidence and growth.

They are:

1. Accept Compliments
2. Discover Your Core Values
3. Embrace Authenticity
4. Know What You Want
5. Discover Your Why
6. Take Action
7. Rewire Your Negative Self-Talk
8. Run Your Own Race
9. Celebrate Small Wins
10. Align Your Breath, Body and Mind
11. Adopt a Growth Mindset
12. Find Your Tribe

And now, here you are standing at the edge of something new.

This isn't the end of a book. It's the beginning of a new chapter in your own life.

One where you stop waiting.

One where you stop hiding.

One where you unshrink yourself.

One where you start living more courageously, more intentionally, and more authentically than ever before.

Because the world doesn't need more perfection.

It needs more people willing to show up with scars, stories, and all.

Whatever You Can Do, Do It Now

Take the trip.

Say the words.

Start the project.

Show up for yourself.

Ask the question.

Offer the idea.

Speak your truth.

Choose your confidence.

Not someday.

Now.

A Moment of Perspective

While I was in the hospital after the fall, I saw a young boy with a broken arm. His mother was working far away, and a neighbor had been caring for him. Because they couldn't afford care, they waited too long to bring him in. By the time he reached the hospital, it was too late. The doctors couldn't save his arm.

It was a heartbreaking reminder of how precious, and sometimes fragile, access to care and support is. I looked around the hospital and saw so many others struggling. Understaffed units. Limited supplies. People in pain.

And I realized just how much I take for granted, and how easily we assume we'll always have time. But we don't.

So if you're reading this now, with breath in your lungs and possibility ahead of you, here's what I want you to hear: **do not waste your one precious life waiting.**

FINAL REFLECTION

- *What have you been waiting to do because it didn't feel urgent?*
- *What small light have you been hiding?*
- *Where can you show up more fully, not later, but now?*
- *Who might be affected by your decision to be brave today?*
- *What's one mini-shift you can make today to bring your confidence, your gifts, your light into the world?*

FINAL NOTE

You were never meant to blend in. You were born to shine.

This is it.

This moment.

This chapter.

This version of you.

This opportunity to choose differently.

Confidence doesn't arrive fully formed. It's not a gift reserved for a lucky few.

It's something you build, practice, stretch into. It's a seed inside you, and now, it's time to water it.

Let the lessons you've read guide you.

Let the stories inspire you.

But more than that, let your life be the proof.

Start where you are.

Use what you have.

Do what you can.

And shine.

Because life truly does happen in a blink.

And you?

You have so much light to give.

Your Voice Matters

Thank you for reading *Unshrink Yourself*. My hope is that these pages have reminded you of your strength, your worth, and the courage that has always been within you.

If this book spoke to your heart or encouraged you in any way, I would be grateful if you could take a moment **to write a review** on any bookstore website. Your words matter, not just to me, but to others who may need the same encouragement you found here.

Together, we can help more people unshrink themselves and step boldly into who they are meant to be.

I appreciate your reviews and look forward to reading them.

With gratitude,
Thanh

Sources Cited

- *Stajkovic, A.D., & Luthans, F. (1998). Self-efficacy and work-related performance: A meta-analysis. Psychological Bulletin.*
- *Bandura, A. (1997). Self-efficacy: The exercise of control. New York: Freeman.*
- *Clance, P.R., & Imes, S.A. (1978). The impostor phenomenon in high achieving women: Dynamics and therapeutic intervention. Psychotherapy: Theory, Research & Practice.*
- *Hewlett-Packard Internal Report (2011).*
- *Kay, K., & Shipman, C. (2014). The Confidence Gap. The Atlantic.*
- *Cuddy, A.J.C. (2012). Your Body Language Shapes Who You Are. TED Talk.*
- *Dweck, C.S. (2006). Mindset: The New Psychology of Success. Random House.*
- *Kandler, C., et al. (2010). Genetic and environmental sources of individual differences in self-esteem: A longitudinal study. Behavior Genetics.*
- *Deci, E. L., & Ryan, R. M. (1985). Intrinsic motivation and self-determination in human behavior. Springer.*
- *Gallup. (2023). State of the global workplace: 2023 report. Gallup, Inc.*
- *Roese, N. J., & Summerville, A. (2005). What we regret most... and why. Personality and Social Psychology Bulletin, 31(9), 1273–1285.*

- *Neff, K. D. (2011). Self-compassion: The proven power of being kind to yourself. William Morrow.*

- *Festinger, L. (1954). A Theory of Social Comparison Processes. Human Relations, 7(2), 117–140.*

- *Lyubomirsky, S., & Ross, L. (1997). Hedonic consequences of social comparison: A contrast of happy and unhappy people. Journal of Personality and Social Psychology, 73(6), 1141–1157.*

- *Vogel, E. A., Rose, J. P., Roberts, L. R., & Eckles, K. (2014). Social comparison, social media, and self-esteem. Psychology of Popular Media Culture, 3(4), 206–222.*

- *Amabile, T. M., & Kramer, S. J. (2011). The Progress Principle: Using Small Wins to Ignite Joy, Engagement, and Creativity at Work. Harvard Business Review Press.*

- *Neff, K. D. (2003). Self-compassion: An alternative conceptualization of a healthy attitude toward oneself. Self and Identity, 2(2), 85–101.*

- *Emmons, R. A., & McCullough, M. E. (2003). Counting blessings versus burdens: An experimental investigation of gratitude and subjective well-being. Journal of Personality and Social Psychology, 84(2), 377–389.*

- *Sheldon, K. M., & Elliot, A. J. (1999). Goal striving, need satisfaction, and longitudinal well-being: The self-concordance model. Journal of Personality and Social Psychology, 76(3), 482–497.*

- *Fardouly, J., Diedrichs, P. C., Vartanian, L. R., & Halliwell, E. (2015). Social comparisons on social media: The impact of Facebook on young women's body image concerns and mood. Body Image, 13, 38–45.*

- *Baumeister, R. F., Bratslavsky, E., Finkenauer, C., & Vohs, K. D. (2001). Bad is stronger than good. Review of General Psychology, 5(4), 323–370.*

- *Killingsworth, M. A., & Gilbert, D. T. (2010). A wandering mind is an unhappy mind. Science, 330(6006), 932.*

- *Watkins, E. R. (2008). Constructive and unconstructive repetitive thought. Annual Review of Clinical Psychology, 4, 285–313.*

- *Amabile, T. M., & Kramer, S. J. (2011). The Progress Principle: Using Small Wins to Ignite Joy, Engagement, and Creativity at Work. Harvard Business Review Press.*

- *Pychyl, T. A. (2013). Solving the Procrastination Puzzle: A Concise Guide to Strategies for Change. TarcherPerigee.*

- *Sarasvathy, S. D. (2001). Causation and effectuation: Toward a theoretical shift from economic inevitability to entrepreneurial contingency. Academy of Management Review, 26(2), 243–263.*

- *Hill, P. L., & Turiano, N. A. (2014). Purpose in life as a predictor of mortality across adulthood. Psychological Science, 25(7), 1482–1486*

- *Yeager, D. S., Henderson, M. D., Paunesku, D., Walton, G. M., D'Mello, S. K., Spitzer, B. J., & Duckworth, A. L. (2014).*

- *Sakulku, J., & Alexander, J. (2011). The impostor phenomenon. International Journal of Behavioral Science, 6(1), 73–92.*

- *Breuning, L. G. (2015). Habits of a Happy Brain: Retrain Your Brain to Boost Your Serotonin, Dopamine, Oxytocin, & Endorphin Levels. Adams Media.*

- *Huberman, A. (2021). Huberman Lab Podcast: How to Stay Motivated. Stanford University School of Medicine.*

- *Harvard Medical School. (2018, June 8). Dopamine and motivation: How the brain reinforces behavior. ScienceDaily.*

- *Schultz, W. (2015). Neuronal reward and decision signals: From theories to data. Physiological Reviews, 95(3), 853–951.*

APPENDIX A:

List of Core Values

In Mini-Shift #2, we talked about discovering our core values. Below is the list of typical values, and guided questions to help you identify your top 5 core values:

- When you are at your best, what values are you living out?
- Which values have helped you during your hardest moments?
- If you could pass down only five values to your children or someone you love, what would they be?
- Which values drive your biggest life decisions—not just what feels good, but what directs your actions?

A	B
Accountability	Balance
Achievement	Beauty
Adventure	Boldness
Ambition	Bravery
Authenticity	Belonging
Autonomy	Being Present
Awareness	Belief

C

Challenge

Clarity

Collaboration

Commitment

Compassion

Competence

Confidence

Connection

Consistency

Contribution

Courage

Creativity

Curiosity

D

Decisiveness

Dependability

Determination

Discipline

Diversity

E

Empathy

Encouragement

Equality

Excellence

Exploration

Expression

F

Fairness

Faith

Family

Flexibility

Forgiveness

Freedom

Friendship

Fun

G

Generosity

Grace

Gratitude

Growth

H

Harmony

Health

Honesty

Honor

Hope

Humility

Humor

I

Impact
Inclusion
Independence
Influence
Ingenuity
Inner Peace
Innovation
Integrity
Intuition

J
Joy
Justice

K
Kindness
Knowledge

L
Leadership
Learning
Legacy
Listening
Love
Loyalty

M
Mindfulness

Meaning
Moderation
Motivation

O
Openness
Optimism
Order
Organization
Ownership

P
Passion
Patience
Peace
Perseverance
Personal Growth
Playfulness
Pleasure
Positivity
Power
Presence
Pride
Purpose

R
Recognition
Reflection

Relationships

Reliability

Resilience

Resourcefulness

Respect

Responsibility

Results

S

Safety

Security

Self-Discipline

Self-Expression

Self-Respect

Service

Simplicity

Spirituality

Stability

Stewardship

Strength

Success

Support

Sustainability

T

Teamwork

Thankfulness

Thoughtfulness

Tolerance

Tradition

Transparency

Trust

Truth

U–Z

Understanding

Uniqueness

Unity

Vision

Vulnerability

Wealth

Wisdom

Wonder

Zeal

Suggested Reading List

1. *The Success Principles: How to Get from Where You Are to Where You Want to Be* by Jack Canfield
2. *Mindset: The New Psychology of Success* by Carol S. Dweck
3. *The Confidence Code: The Science and Art of Self-Assurance – What Women Should Know* by Katty Kay & Claire Shipman
4. *You Are a Badass: How to Stop Doubting Your Greatness and Live an Awesome Life* by Jen Sincero
5. *Can't Hurt Me: Master Your Mind and Defy the Odds* by David Goggins
6. *The Tao of Self-Confidence: A Guide to Moving Beyond Trauma and Awakening the Leader Within* by Sheena Yap Chan
7. *Atomic Habits: An Easy & Proven Way to Build Good Habits & Break Bad Ones* by James Clear
8. *The Let Them Theory* by Mel Robbins

About the Author

Thanh Nguyen is a bestselling author, certified Maxwell Leadership coach, and keynote speaker who helps people live positively and lead courageously. With over two decades of experience in engineering and executive leadership, and as one of the few women of color in her field, Thanh knows firsthand what it's like to navigate self-doubt, overcome cultural and societal expectations, and find her voice in high-stakes spaces.

Originally from Vietnam, Thanh immigrated to the United States as a teenager, not knowing the language and facing enormous challenges. She earned dual graduate degrees in electrical engineering and business administration, holds two U.S. patents, and served as a vice president of engineering before starting her position as a Professor in the Practice at Rice University and founding her own leadership and personal development company, The Encourage Team.

Thanh is the author of the bestselling book *Calm in Chaos: Mindfulness and Meditation for Busy Professionals* (Loving Heart Publishing, 2024), which blends mindfulness with practical tools for thriving in today's fast-paced world. Her work combines science, storytelling, and heart to help others build confidence, find purpose, and create meaningful impact.

www.ingramcontent.com/pod-product-compliance
Lightning Source LLC
Chambersburg PA
CBHW070920130626
46555CB00001B/217